"One of the unfortunate, unir
professionalization of lay ministry since ...
rise of silos separating roles and responsibilities on the parish
staff. *Reweaving the Ministries* offers a biblically centered and
pastorally relevant model for overcoming this compartmentali-
zation. If every ministerial team in the country read this book,
talked about it together, and put it into practice, we would be a
better church for it!"

> —Edward P. Hahnenberg, PhD, is the Breen Chair in
> Catholic Theology at John Carroll University and the
> author of *Theology for Ministry: An Introduction for
> Lay Ministers*

"Ministers of the Christian community—ordained and lay
ecclesial—will benefit greatly from this wise and inspiring
vision of ministry rooted in Ostdiek's biblical, liturgical, and
prophetic imagination. If there is one book your parish staff
reads together this year, make sure it is *Reweaving the Ministries*."

> —Kathleen A. Cahalan
> Professor of Practical Theology
> Saint John's University School of Theology and Seminary

"Ministers today celebrate the post Vatican II explosion of
ministry; they also long for fuller collaboration as our
hierarchical history and growing specialization create silos. How
can we become truly co-workers? Ostdiek's meditative reading
of the Emmaus story explores the ministries of companioning,
Word, table, mystagogy, and mission, and their radical
connection in serving the faith journey of disciples. A theological
frame, probing questions, practical strategies, and spiritual depth
make this an ideal book for ministry leaders to read, ponder, and
practice as they work to *Reweave the Ministries*."

> —Zeni Fox, PhD
> Professor Emerita, Immaculate Conception Seminary,
> Seton Hall University; author, *New Ecclesial Ministry:
> Lay Professionals Serving the Church*

"This is a profound, challenging, and comforting book. Readers will delve into and glory in the riches of church teaching on evolving pastoral ministry. Through the paradigm of Emmaus pastoral ministers are challenged to revisit how they companion people on their journeys of faith, listen again to the Good News, break bread, have their hearts set on fire, and re-engage in mission. Readers take comfort that they are engaging in such rich ministries, not as soloists, but as weavers working together."

—Fr. Robert J. Karris, OFM
St. Bonaventure University

Reweaving the Ministries

The Emmaus Paradigm

Gilbert Ostdiek, OFM

LITURGICAL PRESS

Collegeville, Minnesota

www.litpress.org

1   2   3   4   5   6   7   8   9

Library of Congress Cataloging-in-Publication Data

Names: Ostdiek, Gilbert, author.
Title: Reweaving the ministries : the Emmaus paradigm / Gilbert Ostdiek, OFM.
Description: Collegeville, Minnesota : Liturgical Press, [2021] | Includes bibliographical references. | Summary: "As seen through the Emmaus story, an invitation to those engaged in ministry and those preparing for it to think of their own ministry as part of a larger pastoral tapestry, unfolding from catechesis to Eucharist to mission"— Provided by publisher.
Identifiers: LCCN 2020050471 (print) | LCCN 2020050472 (ebook) | ISBN 9780814666210 (paperback) | ISBN 9780814666470 (epub) | ISBN 9780814666470 (mobi) | ISBN 9780814666470 (pdf)
Subjects: LCSH: Bible. Luke, XXIV, 13-35—Criticism, interpretation, etc. | Pastoral theology—Catholic Church. | Church work—Catholic Church.
Classification: LCC BS2595.52 .O88 2021 (print) | LCC BS2595.52 (ebook) | DDC 253/.32—dc23
LC record available at https://lccn.loc.gov/2020050471
LC ebook record available at https://lccn.loc.gov/2020050472

Contents

Preface

The final editing of this manuscript is being done at a difficult time. We are caught in the throes of the coronavirus pandemic. Our accustomed journey through life is completely overshadowed by clouds of deep distress and myriad fears. Life in the world as we have known it has been abruptly shattered and may never return. What lies ahead of us is unknown.

Our experience is not unlike what the two disciples on the way to Emmaus had experienced. The bright hopes they had once harbored were no more; their lives shattered. But wonder of wonders, their hopes for the future were reborn when a stranger approached and walked with them, listening to their story and helping them piece it back together in a way they had never expected.

Many strangers are appearing in our lives now, as for those disciples, to walk with us and help us on the way to what will be. Reports abound of many going out of their way to companion others in need. The outpouring of spontaneous efforts of total strangers to help others in so many ways in these times of need holds a glimmer of hope for the future. What ministry will be like in the future is unknown. Continuing social distance? Virtual presence to others in a more electronic mode? Fewer face-to-face opportunities for extended time for coordination and planning? What does seem quite likely to continue is the great array of ministries now at work in the church and the need to keep them woven together. Can we not hope this will continue?

In light of that hope, it has seemed wise to go ahead with this book and rely on God's ever-present Spirit to bring to new birth the adaptations in ministry that will surely be needed. The Emmaus story offers us a paradigm and assures us that the risen Lord will not abandon us. He promised to send his Spirit to be our advocate and guide on the way.

Gilbert Ostdiek, OFM
Catholic Theological Union
October 4, 2020

Abbreviations

AA   *Apostolicam Actuositatem*: Decree on the Apostolate of the Laity (Vatican II, November 18, 1965)

AG   *Ad Gentes*: Decree on the Missionary Activity of
the Church (Vatican II, December 7, 1965)

CCC   *Catechism of the Catholic Church* (John Paul II,
1992)

CL   *Christifideles Laici*: Postsynodal Apostolic Exhortation (John Paul II, 1988)

CT   *Catechesi Tradendae*: Apostolic Exhortation on
Catechesis in Our Time (John Paul II, 1979)

DV   *Dei Verbum*: Dogmatic Constitution on Divine
Revelation (Vatican II, November 18, 1965)

EG   *Evangelii Gaudium*: Apostolic Exhortation on the
Proclamation of the Gospel in Today's World
(Francis, 2013)

EN   *Evangelii Nuntiandi*: Apostolic Exhortation (Paul
VI, 1975)

GDC   *General Directory for Catechesis* (Congregation for
the Clergy, 1997)

GIRM   *General Instruction of the Roman Missal* (ICEL
translation, 2010)

GS   *Gaudium et Spes*: Pastoral Constitution on the
Church in the Modern World (Vatican II, December 7, 1965)

LG   *Lumen Gentium*: Dogmatic Constitution on the
Church (Vatican II, November 21, 1964)

MR *Missale Romanum*: The Roman Missal, 3rd edition (ICEL translation, 2010)

NDC *National Directory for Catechesis* (USCCB, 2005)

OM The Order of Mass, *Missale Romanum*, 3rd edition (ICEL translation, 2010)

RCIA *Rite of Christian Initiation of Adults* (ICEL translation, NCCB edition, 1988)

SC *Sacrosanctum Concilium*: The Constitution on the Sacred Liturgy (Vatican II, December 4, 1963)

Introduction

Books sometimes begin without notice, with the first tentative spinning out of an idea. That simple thread of thought gradually takes on a life of its own, and over time it is woven together with many other ideas, like so many multicolored threads interwoven until they come together into a larger pattern. That is the case with this book.

The first threads of the idea were spun in 1987. I was invited to give an address at the annual conference of the Institute of Liturgical Studies at Valparaiso University.[1] The presentation was to address two questions: how is Eucharist related to religious education, on one hand, and to gospel witness, on the other? As I pondered the assignment, it dawned on me that the Emmaus story in Luke's account (Luke 24:13-35) makes those connections in a very compelling way. As the story unfolds, it moves from catechesis to Eucharist and then from Eucharist to mission. In effect, the moment of recognition of the risen Lord at the supper table binds both catechesis and mission together. From that time on, the Emmaus story has gradually threaded its way into my theology courses, adult education workshops, and articles.[2] In the process, it has been interwoven with many

---

1. "What We Have Seen and Heard and Touched," The 1987 Institute of Liturgical Studies Occasional Papers, paper 26, 87–103, https://scholar.valpo.edu/ils_papers/26/.

2. For example, Gil Ostdiek, "The Eucharist and Pastoral Ministry: The Emmaus Paradigm," *Emanuel* 119 (November/December 2013): 487–96.

related areas of pastoral ministry and became a promising paradigm for interweaving them.

It seems to me now that the Emmaus paradigm has much to offer as we face the current task of coordinating the present array of disparate ministries[3] and reweaving them into a more integrated pastoral practice. The ministerial practices under consideration here are not the many one-to-one forms of individual pastoral care but rather those ministries that are offered, whether by an individual minister or by ministerial coworkers, for the community as a whole or for groups within it.

This book reflects on why and how we might envision reweaving those ministries for the future. It has been written primarily as a reflective invitation with three audiences in mind. It is offered first to those now engaged in the ministries or in programs of preparation for them, to invite them to think of their own ministry as part of a larger pastoral tapestry. It is also offered to those in pastoral leadership, together with their staffs, who are charged with the responsibility of envisioning an integrated shape of ministry to a community and coordinating the practice of the ministries, whether on a local parish level or on a higher diocesan level. And finally, it may also serve as a modest conversation starter for those interested in thinking together more broadly about the future shape of pastoral ministry. These pages are written from the limited perspective of a US Roman Catholic liturgist interested in how liturgy relates to the rest of pastoral ministry, in the hope that others may find it useful as well. My fondest hope is that this book may contribute in

---

3. These ministries include not only ordained ministries and official lay ecclesial ministries, which have leadership responsibilities and are often thought of as "pastoral ministries," but also the many kinds of ministries that have sprung up recently. "Pastoral ministry" in the singular will also be used to refer to the ministries as a whole.

some small way to pastoral ministers becoming ever more fully, in St. Paul's apt description, coworkers with one another and, indeed, coworkers with God in the care of God's people.[4]

This book unfolds in the following way. Chapter 1 will look at how ministry in the US Roman Catholic Church today is rapidly taking on a great variety of forms, ordained and lay, offering enticing new possibilities for collaboration between coworkers. The image of reweaving these ministries and the need for that will be explained, and the Emmaus story will be put forward as a promising paradigm for that task. The next five chapters will each take up one of the five phases of the risen Lord's ministry to the two disciples on their journey. The pattern for each of these chapters will be: (1) the account of a ministry moment in the Emmaus story, (2) reflection on the paradigm of ministry modeled there, (3) key intersections connecting the ministries, and (4) particular strategies for a reweaving. The final chapter will revisit the Emmaus story to gather it up into a continuous reflection on the paradigm it offers for reweaving pastoral ministry today. It will conclude with some pastoral considerations for the work of reweaving. Appendixes will provide interested readers some technical notes to three of the chapters and a description of how the Emmaus account was actually used in a workshop for reweaving parish ministries.

I owe a great debt of gratitude to so many who have been coworkers in interweaving the ideas in this book. Theology students, workshop participants, and faculty colleagues at Catholic Theological Union have all had a hand in weaving the threads together over the years since the Valparaiso conference. I owe particular thanks to faculty colleagues

---

4. Paul often uses the word "coworker" (*synergon*) to name his associates and fellow workers in ministry (e.g., Rom 16:3), and in that shared ministry they all are truly coworkers with God (1 Cor 3:9).

C. Vanessa White and Christina Zaker, whose wise advice has immensely improved what is written here. The Franciscan community at St. Peter's Church in the Loop provided warm fraternal hospitality while final editing was being done; for that I am most grateful. Deep thanks are due as well to Liturgical Press for the patient support this project has received and especially to my family from whom I have learned so much about the joy of collaboration. It is my fond hope that these musings may contribute in some small way to current rethinking of what ministry is and how we can weave together the rich array of ministries with which we are blessed.

1
Reweaving the Ministries

Let's begin with a simple admission. Perhaps the title of this book and chapter should end with a question mark. Hidden within this title are several questions. First, about the image of reweaving. Was ministry once woven and then became unwoven? Is it in need of reweaving today? And second, about Emmaus. If we answer yes to those questions, why should we think of using biblical accounts from different historical contexts of a long-ago era and in particular the Emmaus story as an apt model for that reweaving today? What pastoral inspiration and model would it offer us now? Pondering these questions will set the context for the remaining chapters.

Woven to Unwoven

Zeni Fox, well known for her work on lay ministry, offers us a short answer to the first questions about reweaving. She notes that the diverse and changing forms of ministry found in the early church were gradually swallowed up by the ordained ministry and woven into it by the end of the first millennium.[1] Let's unpack that a bit.

---

1. Zeni Fox, "The Intersection of Present Experience and the Tradition," in *New Ecclesial Ministry: Lay Professionals Serving the Church*, rev. and exp. ed. (Franklin, WI: Sheed & Ward, 2002), 299–321, here at 300–304.

Scholars who have studied extensively the pattern of ministry in the early church highlight several features of that ministry.[2] A wide variety of ministries arose quickly. Paul gives three somewhat different lists (1 Cor 12:8-10; 12:28; Eph 4:11). There were other "forms of assistance" (1 Cor 12:28) as well, like the relief collection for the Jerusalem community (1 Cor 16:1; 2 Cor 9:12-13), which surfaced in response to the rise of particular needs. That outburst of ministries to meet the needs of the moment is not unlike what we are experiencing now in the lay ministries. But scholars also warn us against assuming that those early ministries match exactly how we now name the ministries. There was no single pattern. That would begin to take shape only several decades later, toward the end of the first century.

Despite this lack of a single way of naming and organizing this great variety of ministries, there was a strong unity between them that lay far deeper. They all come from the same trinitarian source: spiritual gifts from the Spirit, forms of service from the Lord, and workings from God (1 Cor 12:4-6). They are all given for a single purpose: "To each is given the manifestation of the Spirit for the common good" (1 Cor 12:7). And they are given to everyone to "equip the saints [the people of God] for the work of ministry [*diakonia*], for building up the body of Christ" (Eph 4:12).

The early church presents a truly collaborative vision for ministry: (1) a unity of many ministries all tied to one mission; (2) ministries that match the gifts God gives in response to the changing needs of God's people; and (3) ministers who collaborate as coworkers in carrying out the mission of

---

2. For fuller biblical and doctrinal discussion of the early shaping of ministry, see, respectively, Daniel J. Harrington, *The Church According to the New Testament: What the Wisdom and Witness of Early Christianity Teach Us Today* (Lanham, MD: Sheed & Ward, 2001), 145–73, and Walter Kasper, *The Catholic Church: Nature, Reality and Mission*, trans. Thomas Hoebel (New York: Bloomsbury, T & T Clark, 2015), 219–46.

God in the world. "Throughout the ages the holy Spirit makes the entire church 'one in communion and ministry; and provides her with different hierarchical and charismatic gifts,' . . . inspiring in the hearts of the faithful that same spirit of mission which impelled Christ himself" (AG 4).[3]

Skip forward a millennium and note with Zeni Fox that the diverse and changing forms of lay ministry found in the early church were gradually swallowed up by the ordained ministry and woven into it by the end of the first millennium.[4] Over the centuries before Vatican II ministry had come to be understood "as a singular reality, vested in its fullness in the bishops"[5] and in priests as "co-workers of the order of bishops."[6] On the eve of the council there was some limited lay involvement through associations such as the Legion of Mary and Catholic Action, under the rubric of the "apostolate of the laity." It was clear, especially in Catholic Action, that laypersons did not have a ministry that was uniquely and rightfully their own. They were simply seen as lay auxiliaries allowed to assist in the work of the ordained ministers. Lay apostolic activity, carried out under the authorization and guidance of the clergy, was a derivative form of participation in the ordained ministry. Ordination was thus assumed to be the sole foundation of ministry. That close-knit ordination-based pattern was about to become unwoven as the Second Vatican Council opened it up for a new reweaving.

Why a Reweaving Now?

It is no secret that the shape of ministry in the Roman Church has been undergoing a major shift in the decades since Vatican II. Three key factors merit brief consideration.

---

3. Appendix 3 at the end of the book has more on this.
4. Zeni Fox, *New Ecclesial Ministry*, 304.
5. Zeni Fox, *New Ecclesial Ministry*, 300.
6. The homily in the 2003 Rite of Ordination of Priests, 123.

Proliferation

First, the most dramatic development has been a veritable explosion of lay involvement in ministry since Vatican II. Numerous lay ministers are now increasingly at work alongside ordained ministers.

The story of how the solid foundations laid at the council[7] opened the way to this accelerating proliferation is fascinating. Only a few milestones can be named here.[8] The ministries of lector and acolyte, formerly minor orders for clergy, were opened to laity in 1972.[9] A year later laypersons were allowed to distribute Holy Communion as Extraordinary Eucharistic Ministers,[10] and ten years after that laypersons were authorized to exercise ministries in other instances.[11] Finally, this growing experience of lay ministry led to a synod in 1987 to reflect on the "Vocation and Mission of the

---

7. Especially the Dogmatic Constitution on the Church (*Lumen Gentium*), 1964, full membership of the baptized in the People of God and the universal call to holiness (chapters 2, 4, 5); and the Decree on the Apostolate of the Laity (*Apostolicam Actuositatem*), 1965, a comprehensive understanding of the role of the laity and how it is exercised. Two other documents that same year, the Decree on the Church's Mission (*Ad Gentes*) and the Pastoral Constitution on the Church in the Modern World (*Gaudium et Spes*), added a broader understanding of the church's mission to transformation of the world, opening further possibilities for lay involvement.

8. What follows is only a summary of some highlights. For more extensive treatment, see Aurelie A. Hagstrom, *The Emerging Laity: Vocation, Mission, and Spirituality* (New York: Paulist Press, 2010); Dolores R. Leckey, *The Laity and Christian Education* (New York: Paulist Press, 2006).

9. Paul VI, Apostolic Letter *Ministeria Quaedam*, 1972.

10. Congregation for the Discipline of the Sacraments, *Immensae Caritatis*, 1973.

11. *Code of Canon Law*, c. 228–30, 910, revised in 1983. The *Code* allows laypersons "to exercise the ministry of the word, to preside over liturgical prayers, to confer baptism, and to distribute Holy Communion in accord with the prescriptions of the law" (c. 230.3). Such authorization may be subject to regulations of episcopal conferences and the local diocese.

Laity in the Church and in the World." The pope's postsynodal apostolic exhortation[12] summed up and further developed the conciliar teaching on the call and mission of the laity.[13] The synod and *Christifideles Laici* affirmed and gave further impetus to the growth of lay ministry.

At about that same time, the language of "lay ecclesial ministry" was coming into more frequent use.[14] Within the larger group of lay ministers, this description came to refer to a particular group of those who have received official authorization by the hierarchy to serve publicly in positions of leadership in the local church; who work in mutual collaboration with the bishops, priests, and deacons; and who had undergone appropriate preparation and formation.[15] Those now identified with the official title of lay ecclesial minister (LEM) in a given diocese typically include pastoral associates, directors of catechesis and faith formation, leaders of youth ministry, school principals, and directors of liturgy or pastoral music.

At this point let's pause and take a quick look at some numbers. In 2018 the number of lay ecclesial ministers

12. John Paul II, *Christifideles Laici*, 1987. For a helpful summary and analysis of this papal document, see Peter N. V. Hai, "Reflections on John Paul II's Theology of the Laity: 20th Anniversary of *Christifideles Laici* (1989)," http://www.vatican.va/content/john-paul-ii/en/apost _exhortations/documents/hf_jp-ii_exh_30121988_christifideles-laici .html.

13. Notably, in place of the conciliar definition of the laity by "what they are not" (LG 31), this document proposed a positive definition, i.e., those who through baptism are made one body with Christ, established among the people of God, and made sharers in the priestly, prophetic, and kingly office of Christ and also in the mission of the whole church (CL 9–17).

14. Already in 1980 the USCCB used the language of "lay ecclesial ministry." See their *Called and Gifted: The American Catholic Laity* (Washington, DC: USCCB, 1980), 3–4.

15. See USCCB, *Co-Workers in the Vineyard of the Lord* (Washington, DC USCCB, 2005), 10–13.

(including vowed religious) in parish ministry, such as the roles just named, had reached 39,651, outnumbering the 36,580 priests.[16] In 2018 and 2019 the number of graduate-level seminarians was 3,526,[17] while lay ecclesial ministry program enrollments numbered 16,585 in 2018,[18] outnumbering the seminarians 4.9 to one. Without doubt a dramatic change in the face of ministry is well underway and ongoing.

This wider involvement of the laity in ministry, however, extends well beyond the LEMs. Many others are involved in ministries within a parish, such as marriage preparation, catechesis, bereavement, and communion for the homebound. In addition, the final document of Vatican II, the Pastoral Constitution on the Church in the Modern World (*Gaudium et Spes*), had planted seeds for a vastly expanded vision of the mission of the church. In addition to internal service to the church itself, that mission could now entail service to all facets of life in the world of today, social, economic, and political. Under the theme of evangelization, subsequent pronouncements of the popes, especially Paul VI, John Paul II, and Francis, have forcefully proclaimed that the mission of the church includes the pursuit of justice, peace, care of the earth, and the transformation of the world. It is especially within this expanded vision that so many of the laity, often with the sup-

16. Georgetown Center for Applied Research in the Apostolate (CARA), https://cara.georgetown.edu/frequently-requested-church-statistics/ (accessed 8-2-2020).

17. CARA, "Catholic Ministry Formation Enrollment: Statistical Overview for 2018–2019," 2–3 and 11, https://cara.georgetown.edu/Statistical Overview201819.pdf. The figures given here, which include graduate pre-theology and theology, differ slightly from the total of 3,353 in FAQs.

18. CARA, "Catholic Ministry Formation Enrollment," 27. On the following page, CARA notes wide fluctuations in this category over the years due to variations in the number of programs and the percentages of those reporting (e.g., the ratio fell from 4.9 to 3.6 a year later because 14 of the LEM programs did not report, and three years earlier LEM enrollment had reached a high of 23,681).

port of their parish and under its umbrella, have taken up their role in mission and invested their energies in it.[19]

In God's providence and under the inspiration of the Holy Spirit, this proliferation of lay ministries has been a great gift to the church. As the number of priests active in ministry has continued to decline, many laypeople have answered the call to serve in a wide variety of ministries, official and unofficial. Vatican II had laid the foundations for opening up new and wider pathways into ministry.

Two significant changes have resulted. Clearly the face of ministry has changed through this proliferation of lay ministries, official and unofficial, and will likely continue to do so. Second, the understanding of ministry itself has also been transformed. Prior to Vatican II a sharp dividing line had been drawn between clergy and laity. Ministry in the proper sense belonged to the clergy in virtue of their ordination. After Vatican II, ministry opened up to the laity in virtue of their baptism. The top-down "dividing line" model gave way to a circular "community of ministries" model.[20] Accordingly, the language of ministry, rooted theologically in baptism and discipleship, has become much broader: "*Christian ministry is any activity, done on behalf of the church community, that proclaims, celebrates, and serves the reign of God.*"[21] In addition to this proliferation, two more major factors need to be added briefly.

19. One might see this Spirit-led expansion of ministry beyond the internal needs of the church as remarkably similar to the Spirit-inspired outburst of ministries in the early church.

20. For an account of the historical background of this dramatic transformation in the understanding of ministry and the shifts in theology to which it led, see Thomas F. O'Meara, *Theology of Ministry: Completely Revised Edition* (New York: Paulist Press, 1999), 5–34; Edward P. Hahnenberg, *Ministries: A Relational Approach* (New York: Crossroad Publishing Company / A Herder & Herder Book, 2003), 1–38.

21. Edward P. Hahnenberg, *Theology for Ministry: An Introduction for Lay Ministers* (Collegeville, MN: Liturgical Press, 2014), 109 (emphasis original).

Professionalization

To the proliferation of ministry and the expanded vision it entailed we now need to add a second major factor, the professionalization of these emerging ministries. As the ministries for laypeople have become established and grown, many initiatives have been taken to identify their professional status and guide their professional development. Among these is the formation of professional organizations,[22] an umbrella organization for certification of LEMs,[23] and a number of USCCB publications.[24] Organizations and documents such as these clearly attest to the growing professionalization of lay ministries in this country.

Specialization

This is the final factor to consider. Proliferation and professionalization of the ministries have resulted in practitioners of these multiple ministries focusing more narrowly on their particular areas of expertise and responsibility. This sense

22. The National Association of Catholic Chaplains (NACC, 1965); the National Conference for Catechetical Leadership (NCCL, 1967); the Federation of Diocesan Liturgical Commissions (FDLC, 1969); the National Association for Pastoral Musicians (NPM, 1976); the National Association of Lay Ministries (NALM, 1976); the National Federation for Catholic Youth Ministry (NFCYM, 1982); and the Catholic Campus Ministry Association (CCMA, 1985).

23. The Alliance for the Certification of Lay Ecclesial Ministry (ACLEM). See USCCB Subcommittee on Certification for Ecclesial Ministry and Service, *Certification Handbook*, https://www.usccb.org/beliefs-and-teachings/how-we-teach/catholic-education/certification/upload/-Certification-Handbook-2016.pdf; also the *National Certification Standards for Ecclesial Lay Ministers* (Washington, DC: NALM et al., 2006). This official ordering of some lay ministries could be seen as reminiscent of institutionalization of ministries that soon occurred in the early church.

24. Especially *Co-Workers in the Vineyard of the Lord: A Resource for Guiding the Development of Lay Ecclesial Ministry* (Washington, DC: USCCB, 2005).

of ministerial specialization is bolstered by several other factors.[25] One is the widespread development of graduate degree programs of preparation for specific ministries. Another is the formation of the Alliance for the Certification of Lay Ecclesial Ministry and the development of the *Certification Handbook* and the *Official Standards: National Certification Standards for Ecclesial Lay Ministers*, noted above. Still another is the USCCB comprehensive guide for the development of lay ecclesial ministry, *Co-Workers in the Vineyard of the Lord*, also cited above. Such specialization can tend to isolate the ministries from each other, leading at times to a reluctance to cross over into other areas of ministry and to a neglect of collaboration and an integrated pastoral approach to ministry. It is especially this risk of an unintended scattering of the ministries into self-contained "siloes" that now calls for paying careful attention to coordination and collaboration, for an intentional and coordinated reweaving of these ministries.

A Biblical Model

In the face of the need for such a fundamental rethinking of current pastoral practice as it is now being reshaped, a typical Christian instinct is to return to the Scriptures for a vision and model. Such biblical resources include the ministry of Jesus himself and in particular the Emmaus story. To those we now turn.

The Ministry of Jesus

At the beginning of this chapter we posed a second question. Can we use biblical accounts from particular historical

---

25. For a fuller discussion, see Kathleen A. Cahalan, *Introducing the Practice of Ministry* (Collegeville, MN: Liturgical Press, 2010), 126–29.

contexts of a long-ago era as models for ministry today? Can the ministry of Jesus be a model for ministry today? Biblical scholar Seán Kealy and others have wrestled with that very question.[26] In the numerous books and articles on this question authors cite aspects of the ministry of Jesus as just such a model for current ministries. After surveying the models prevalent in Judaism at the time of Jesus, Kealy notes that Jesus does not follow any one of them exclusively. Rather he drew on several of them to address various situations. Even so, Kealy accepts that "the basic options and tendencies of the human condition in Jesus' day were not that different from our own. . . . [A] closer analysis shows that men and women of the Bible are remarkably close to us in their joys, their hopes and fears, their doubts, trouble and anguish."[27] Kealy does not, however, opt for deriving detailed blueprints for current ministries from the ministry of Jesus. Rather, Kealy stresses several characteristics of the mission and ministry of Jesus that became foundational for the early church and that remain decisive for mission and ministry today. Here are some such characteristics.[28]

- *God's mission.* Total commitment to doing God's will is the hallmark of the Jewish spirituality inherited by Jesus. The words Jesus spoke and the deeds he performed were only those given him by the one who sent him (John 12:49; 5:19). Carrying out God's saving plan, under the guidance and power of the Spirit (Luke 4:1, 14), was the mission of Jesus. The command of love at the heart of that plan was woven throughout his ministry. Reliance on God's saving plan and unwavering

---

26. Seán P. Kealy, "Is Jesus a Model for Ministry?," *Irish Theological Quarterly* 55, no. 4 (December 1989): 253–76. Kealy, professor emeritus at Duquesne University and recognized expert on the gospels and the history of biblical scholarship, died in 2018.

27. Kealy, "Is Jesus a Model," 258.

28. Inspired by Kealy, "Is Jesus a Model," 271.

commitment to carrying it out remains the foundation and goal of ministry now.

- *Discernment and boundary crossing.* What God willed, however, had to be discerned concretely in what Jesus experienced in his encounters. For example, his initial working principle was that he was sent "only to the lost sheep of the house of Israel," but the great faith of the Syrophoenician woman, a Gentile, led Jesus to cure her daughter (Mark 7:24-30; Matt 15:24, 26-28) and to cross beyond those original boundaries. He learned to read the specific needs of those he encountered. The mission he entrusted to his disciples was to be universal in scope (Matt 28:19; Luke 24:47). It also calls for discernment, as it did for Jesus, in responding to the needs of people encountered in specific contexts. This kind of boundary breaking is witnessed now in the lay outreach ministries emerging in response to needs and issues of our own times.[29]

- *Urgency and collaboration.* Jesus had a great sense of urgency about carrying out his mission. The ripened harvest had to be gathered lest it be lost (John 4:34-37; Matt 9:38; Luke 10:2). That is why Jesus first sent the Twelve out to proclaim the kingdom and heal the sick (Luke 9:1-2), after they had become familiar with his message, followed by another seventy(-two) disciples (Luke 10:1-20) as coworkers to expand his mission. That same sense of urgency to spread God's love to our world is imperative now. Jesus' example of sending them in pairs, as coworkers, remains a standard for us today, because the task of transforming the world by witnessing to that healing and forgiving love is so great. It is one's own encounter with Jesus as the embodiment of that love which feeds that same sense of

---

29. This Spirit-inspired growth of lay ministries beyond the internal needs of the church is a wonderful complement to the lay ecclesial ministries being drawn into the more structured internal ministries to the church.

urgency in his disciples now, making them all "missionary disciples."[30]

- *Inclusivity and hospitality.* Finally, inclusivity, respectful listening, and hospitable acceptance of people are threaded throughout the ministry of Jesus. Think of his meal parables about life in God's reign and especially his own meal practice. That practice led to the charge his adversaries leveled against him: "This fellow welcomes sinners and eats with them" (Luke 15:2). In times such as ours, can we place limits to God's invitation when God doesn't?

Those characteristics so prominently manifested in the ministry of Jesus are subtly interwoven in the Emmaus story. To that story we now turn.

The Emmaus Paradigm

How can we name the integrated vision of pastoral ministry contained in the Emmaus story? One way is to trace the flow of the ministerial actions of the stranger from scene to scene.[31] He began by joining the two disciples and walking with them on the way (Luke 24:15), listening to them and inviting them to tell once again the story of their experience (v. 19). When their story was finished, when they had told

30. Pope Francis I, Apostolic Exhortation *Evangelii Gaudium* 120, http://www.vatican.va/content/francesco/en/apost_exhortations/documents/papa-francesco_esortazione-ap_20131124_evangelii-gaudium.html.

31. For other ways of outlining the Emmaus story, see O. Kenneth Walther, "A Solemn One Way Trip Becomes a Joyous Roundtrip! A Study of the Structure of Luke 24:13-35," *Ashland Theological Journal* (Fall 1981): 60–87, or the literary-critical analysis of "five concentric circles" by Arthur J. Just Jr., *The Ongoing Feast: Table Fellowship and Eschatology at Emmaus* (Collegeville, MN: Liturgical Press, 1993); or the pastoral approach of Langford, *God Moments: Why Faith Really Matters to a New Generation* (Maryknoll, NY: Orbis, 2001), 186–94, who names them walking with, listening to, talking with, breaking bread with, and empowering.

all of it, he retold their story and gave it a new ending (v. 26), interpreting it through the lens of the Scriptures so familiar to them (v. 27). Accepting their invitation to join them at table, he became the host and led them in the ritual of the breaking of the bread (v. 30). When they recognized him in that action, he vanished from their sight (v. 31), leaving them enabled to name their experience with the stranger (v. 32) and empowered and eager to go back and tell the others (vv. 33-35). In current terminology of pastoral theology, the story has unfolded through several moments or stages, each with its own need for a particular form of ministering to the two disciples:

walking with and listening to them (vv. 15-24)	– *pastoral companioning*
opening up the scripture for them (vv. 25-27)	– *ministry of the word*
breaking bread with them at table (v. 30)	– *liturgy*
naming the fire burning in their hearts (v. 32)	– *mystagogy*
going back to tell the others (vv. 33-35)	– *mission*

The Emmaus story thus provides us with a remarkable paradigm for a larger, more integrated vision of collaborative pastoral ministry in which the particular needs discerned in each stage in the journey of disciples call for weaving the individual ministries of the moment into an integral pastoral care for the whole journey.[32]

---

32. In keeping with the Emmaus narrative, our focus will be on these five ministries. Those in other ministries are invited to find their ministries in the story as well, e.g., the many forms of current mission facing issues in today's world.

Those five phases of ministry on the journey of the two disciples are tightly bound together in two ways. From one angle, the five ministerial actions of the stranger mark phases in the unfolding journey of the disciples. Those acts of ministry do not stand alone, disconnected from one another. Rather, they simply mark a series of turning points or transitional stages on one continuous journey from loss of hope and nascent faith, to full Easter faith and rebirth of hope, and ultimately to mission. Each stage prepares the way for the next one; each stage builds on what has gone before. All lead to and are tied together by mission, their common goal.

From another angle, it is one and the same person, the stranger, who accompanies the two disciples on that journey and performs different forms of ministerial service in response to the need of the moment. This invites us to think of ourselves working together as a cohort of stand-ins for the stranger, the guise he now wears. Current theology holds that we ought to think of ministry not as a noun, as something we each possess, but rather as a verb, an action that we each do in the name of Christ,[33] as the Body of Christ carrying on his mission on this earth.[34] All ministry is derivative from his, done in his name and only by the power of his Spirit. Ministers are simply earthen vessels for that God-given power (2 Cor 4:7). On both counts, then—one and the same minister who ministers to the one journey of the disciples unfolding in its significant phases—the journey narrated in Luke 24 forms one continuous whole.

---

33. Recent tradition has accustomed us to think of the priest as "acting in the person of Christ." Early Christian tradition applied that same phrase to the role of the deacon. The *Catechism of the Catholic Church* notes that in catechesis it is Christ alone who teaches and that all others teach to the extent that they are his spokespersons, enabling Christ to teach with their lips (CCC 427).

34. A poem attributed to Teresa of Avila is worth meditating on: "Christ has no body now but yours" (search online by title).

Seen from that perspective, we need to read the story backward. The disciples would never have gone back to tell the others (mission) if they had not been able to name the burning they had experienced in their hearts (mystagogy); that would not have happened if they had not recognized the stranger at table (liturgy) as the risen Lord and themselves as still his disciples whom he had earlier sent on mission; that would not have happened if their hearts had not been set on fire by a new way of telling their story (ministry of word); and that would not have happened if they had not first been able to unburden themselves completely of their old story of lost faith and shattered hope (pastoral companioning).[35] Each of these forms of ministry builds on those that have gone before; none of them is able of itself to send the disciples back on mission to tell the others the story of what had happened on the road. Here we see a remarkable paradigm for reweaving our growing diversity of ministries into a whole tapestry. To succeed, they each need and build on the ministries that have gone before them. Coworkers, indeed.

An important strategy to help accomplish this goal of reweaving the ministries into one whole yet multihued tapestry is to keep them always in relation to each other. A number of years ago an article by Thomas Morris, well known for his writing on the RCIA, made an intriguing and thought-provoking suggestion. In preparing for the celebration of the catechumenal rite of acceptance, he wrote that at the appropriate time we should

> begin to ask the catechetical and liturgical questions. The catechetical question: What needs to happen in order to celebrate this rite with authenticity? How do I construct

---

35. The process then returns to where it began, for return of the two disciples on mission would not have happened if the stranger himself had not first been sent on mission to be their pastoral companion. One might hear echoes of a similar sequence in Romans 10:14-15.

catechetical gatherings that lead candidates to the point where they can celebrate this rite with integrity and some knowledge? From this vantage point, one can construct gatherings during the pre-catechumenate that are moving toward the rite of acceptance. Then there is no need to rehearse rites. Instead, we lead people to the celebration of the rite.

The liturgical question: How will we celebrate this rite? What are the needs of this community as we celebrate this rite? How do we best adapt the rite to correspond to those needs? Why do we make these adaptations?[36]

In the chapters that follow, we will adopt Morris's strategy and broaden it to include not only those two questions but also questions for each of the ministries portrayed in the Emmaus narrative. We will look at each of those ministries in turn, to ask how they can work together with the other ministries in forming and nurturing disciples for their calling to witness to the gospel and the coming of God's reign. After all, that mission of going to "tell others" is at the very heart of discipleship; it is nonnegotiable. As a faculty colleague has put it, disciples are called to be sent; they are co-missioned.[37] In that same vein, Pope Francis has also written: "Every Christian is a missionary to the extent that he or she has encountered the love of God in Christ Jesus: we no longer say that we are 'disciples' and 'missionaries,' but rather that we are always 'missionary disciples.'"[38]

36. Thomas H. Morris, "Liturgical Catechesis Revisited," *Catechumenate* 17, no. 3 (May 1994): 12–19, here at 16.

37. Anthony J. Gittins, *Called to Be Sent: Co-Missioned as Disciples Today* (Liguori, MO: Liguori Publications, 2008).

38. Pope Francis, Apostolic Exhortation *Evangelii Gaudium* 120.

2
Companioning

Emmaus Story

[13]Now on that same day two of them were going to a village called Emmaus, about seven miles from Jerusalem, [14]and talking with each other about all these things that had happened. [15]While they were talking and discussing, Jesus himself came near and went with them, [16]but their eyes were kept from recognizing him. [17]And he said to them, "What are you discussing with each other while you walk along?" They stood still, looking sad. [18]Then one of them, whose name was Cleopas, answered him, "Are you the only stranger in Jerusalem who does not know the things that have taken place there in these days?" [19]He asked them, "What things?" They replied, "The things about Jesus of Nazareth, who was a prophet mighty in deed and word before God and all the people, [20]and how our chief priests and leaders handed him over to be condemned to death and crucified him. [21]But we had hoped that he was the one to redeem Israel. Yes, and besides all this, it is now the third day since these things took place. [22]Moreover, some women of our group astounded us. They were at the tomb early this morning, [23]and when they did not find his body there, they came back and told us that they had indeed seen a vision of angels who said that he was alive. [24]Some of those who were with us went to the tomb and found it just as the women had said, but they did not see him."[1]

1. The Gospel according to Luke 24:13-24, *New Revised Standard Version* (Division of Christian Education of the National Council of the Churches

Paradigm for Ministry

The first verses (Luke 24:13-14) set the scene, using prepositions (*from* and *to*) to name the point of departure and the
intended destination of their journey and to frame it. As is
so often the case in human experience, the physical journey
of people embodies within it an inward journey of their
spirits and their sense of themselves. It is a heart-wrenching
journey *from* an all-consuming great hope and a fragile initial faith in a Messiah who would free Israel from Roman
occupation *to* total loss of hope and faith and a precipitous
flight back to the life they had left behind to follow him.
Ironically, though they are "on the road" (vv. 32, 35), they
are abandoning "the way."[2] They were feeling not just a
fleeting sadness but a deep distress. That is why they come
to a sudden stand-still, "looking sad,"[3] when the stranger
asks the first question.

The first phase in the stranger's ministry to the two disciples (vv. 15-24) begins as he joins them and walks with them
on the road. Here it is being called "companioning." It could
be named in other ways as well.[4] The first important thing
the stranger does is to walk with them (to walk with or accompany are also fitting ways to name this phase). To walk
with the two disciples in their distress is already an act of

---

of Christ of the Unites States of America, 1989). Unless otherwise noted,
all Scripture quotations are taken from the NRSV and the verse numbers
in parentheses refer to Luke 24:13-35.

2. The same Greek word, *hodos*, is used in both verses 32 and 35. The
earliest name for Christians was followers of "the way," *hodos* (e.g., Acts
9:2).

3. The word *skythrōpos*, translated as "looking sad," can also mean
looking grim-faced, gloomy, dejected.

4. In *Evangelii Gaudium* 169, Pope Francis calls it "the art of accompaniment" required of all: "The Church will have to initiate everyone—priests,
religious and laity—into this 'art of accompaniment' which teaches us to
remove our sandals before the sacred ground of the other (cf. *Ex* 3:5)."

companioning. It implies willingness to join their journey, a readiness to enter into something of what they are feeling.

The act of companioning others that Jesus practiced on the road to Emmaus has a number of important aspects. The first is the simple bodily act of joining the disciples on their journey and walking with them. To walk where they walk is an unspoken act of solidarity and identification with them. The stranger's identification with the two disciples is shown graphically in the image on the cover of this book. That bas-relief sculpture adorns one pier of the cloister ambulatory connected to the abbey church of Santo Domingo de Silos on the medieval pilgrimage route to Santiago de Compostela. Pilgrims on the way to Compostela were welcomed at the abbey for overnight lodging. The figure of the stranger on the right is dressed in the garb of a barefoot medieval pilgrim, with short staff and a satchel at his waist. If you look closely, you can detect a pilgrim's shell attached to the satchel. A large scallop shell, used as both cup and plate on the journey, was the badge of pilgrims walking to Compostela (it remains so to this day). That shell and his garb identify the risen Jesus as a fellow pilgrim not only with the two disciples but also with medieval pilgrims on the way to Compostela as one with them on their journey (and indeed with subsequent pilgrims of every time and place).[5]

---

5. One might wonder why the unknown sculptor at Santo Domingo chose to dress the stranger in the garb of an early twelfth-century pilgrim to Compostela. The Greek verb in Luke 24:28 translated as "stranger" is *paroikeis* (present participle of *paroikéō*), to be a resident alien, sojourner, foreigner, stranger, visitor. The meanings of the Latin Vulgate and Spanish texts to which the sculptor most likely had access were similar: Latin (*peregrinus*; stranger, alien, foreigner, wanderer) or Spanish (*el peregrino*; traveler, wayfarer, stranger, foreigner) are similar in meaning to the Greek, but in both cases "pilgrim" is one of their first meanings. The sculptor deftly connects the stranger to companions returning from the pilgrimage feast of Passover in Jerusalem and with medieval pilgrims on the way to Compostela.

The next important aspect of companioning is listening (another way to name this phase of ministry). Notice also that the stranger's head is turned attentively to the two in the Emmaus bas-relief. And so, he asks his first question: "What are you discussing?" (v. 17). When they answer "the things" that have just taken place in Jerusalem, he simply asks a second question: "What things?" (v. 19). What we witness here are two of the most important questions one can ask in any ministry. Both questions are asked in a neutral, open-ended way. They invite others to name what is going on and to tell their story. They promise an empathetic hearing without pre-judgment. That is just what the stranger does. He listens to the distressing story of the experience for which they can find no meaning. He allows them to tell their story to its bitter end without interruption, until they have told the all of it and know that it has been truly heard, that they need not tell it again. Only then, experience tells us, will it be possible for them to hear a new way of telling the same story but with a different ending and new meaning.

Such attentive listening is the kind of attitude and way of dealing with people that Jesus had shown early on and throughout his public ministry. Think of the young Jesus in the temple "sitting among the teachers, listening to them and asking them questions" (Luke 2:46). Or remember how Jesus listens to the accusations of adultery that scribes and Pharisees are casting at a woman. As he silently writes on the ground they go away one by one, and he gently asks her a question before sending her away without recrimination (John 8:3-13). There are many such stories of how Jesus listens and engages in conversations with those he meets, like the Samaritan woman at the well (John 4:4-42).[6]

---

6. For an insightful commentary, see Sandra M. Schneiders, *The Revelatory Text: Interpreting the New Testament as Sacred Scripture*, 2nd ed. (Collegeville, MN: Liturgical Press, 1999), 180–99.

In the Emmaus story the stranger does not merely hear them; he pays full attention to what they have to say. That kind of listening requires an inner attitude of attentive silence, of letting others speak and focusing attentively on the inner experience of the story they have to tell. This is not just listening with the ears. In the prologue to his Rule, St. Benedict instructs young monks about how they are to listen to the instructions of their master. He counsels: "Listen carefully . . . and attend to them with the ear of your heart."[7] Listening with the "ear of the heart" is a different kind of listening, surely appropriate in any ministry. If the heart is at the core of our person and our capacity to receive and give love, then this kind of listening attends primarily not to ideas and their logic but to the story of people's relationships and loves[8] and, yes, to their stories of hurt and loss as well. In effect, walking with others and listening to them is a lovingly attentive presence forgetful of self; it is an empathetic offer to enter into the story of their experience.

With those ideas in mind, we return to the Emmaus story. What did the two tell the stranger about what they had experienced in Jerusalem "in these days" (Luke 24:18)? Those days were Passover week in Jerusalem, a pilgrimage feast for which all the people gathered to remember and renew the covenant. It was a time of high messianic expectations. For Jesus and his band it came at the end of the long teaching journey (Luke 9:51–21:36), during his final week of ministry in Jerusalem (21:37–23:56). The story the two disciples tell summarizes the ministry of Jesus, from initial acceptance to later rejections, finally leading to his death. Their

---

7. Timothy Fry, ed., *RB 1980: The Rule of Saint Benedict in English* (Collegeville, MN: Liturgical Press, 2018), Prologue.

8. Janet Martin Soskice, *The Kindness of God: Metaphor, Gender, and Religious Language* (New York: Oxford University Press, 2008), 7–34. I am thankful to Stephen Bevans, a faculty colleague, for calling this work to my attention.

story had a bitter ending: "we had hoped that he was the one to redeem Israel" (24:21).

What were those hopes? As they had approached Jerusalem with Jesus, he told them the parable of the ten gold coins "because he was near Jerusalem, and because *they supposed that the kingdom of God was to appear immediately*" (Luke 19:11; emphasis added). Denis McBride reflects poignantly on what the stranger listening so attentively would have heard in their story. "The disciples' story is told in the language of failure, disappointment and hurt bewilderment. They tell the story from the point of view of its failure, and if people are affected by the significant stories they tell, then the disciples see themselves in terms of their story: they are ex-followers of a prophet, with left-over lives, and nowhere to go but away."[9] That is what they are doing. What else is there to do but go away when life feels that way?

Listening attentively to the stories people have to tell, like the stranger did for the two disciples on the way to Emmaus, is where all ministries should start; it is "the first movement of any kind of care."[10] To put it another way, such walking with and listening to others is an act of hospitality, of receiving and hosting them.[11] The stranger's gift of hospitality and respectful acceptance of the story of their experience opens their emptied-out hearts to hearing and accepting another version of their story as they walk with him on the way. Before turning again to that new story, we need to add a cautionary note.

---

9. Denis McBride, *The Gospel of Luke: A Reflective Commentary* (Northport, NY: Costello, 1982), 317–18.

10. Herbert Anderson and Edward Foley, *Mighty Stories, Dangerous Rituals: Weaving Together the Human and the Divine* (San Francisco, CA: Jossey-Bass Publishers, 1998), 45.

11. See the reflections on listening and hospitality in Emma J. Justes, *Hearing Beyond the Words: How to Become a Listening Pastor* (Nashville, TN: Abingdon Press, 2006), 1-19. This harkens back to the inclusivity and hospitality identified in chapter 1 as characteristic of the ministry of Jesus.

Listening attentively to people's stories in pastoral ministry also brings with it the responsibility to respect appropriate boundaries and to safeguard confidentiality. There are times when the kind of pastoral companioning envisioned here uncovers much deeper needs, needs that call for more extensive pastoral or psychological counseling, spiritual direction, bereavement and grief work, etc. In cases where that kind of expertise is beyond the one who is listening to the story, an absolutely necessary part of responsible pastoral listening is to recognize the limits of one's own capabilities, to be informed about the professional resources available locally that can address those needs, and to make the appropriate referrals. Responsible pastoral listening to personal accounts also demands maintaining a respectful, unwavering confidentiality.

The listening under consideration here, however, concerns experience that is not just individual and private but rather shared by others in some way, such as the feeling of helplessness in face of public disasters such as massive floods, forest fires, or pandemic.[12] Certainly their loss of hope was shared not only by these two disciples but also by others of their small band (24:22, 24) and, indeed, by all the disciples who had accompanied Jesus to Jerusalem with such high hopes (Luke 19:11). In the mind of the two disciples, it was also known to everyone in Jerusalem (24:20).[13] The things that had happened in Jerusalem that week (v. 18)

---

12. More difficult circumstances, such as systemic violence and the attendant depersonalization of peoples, which call for a more demanding process of social reconciliation, have given rise to a special form of listening. The process begins with what some call "listening circles" or "healing circles," e.g., Robert J. Schreiter, "Entering the Healing Circle: The Practice of Reconciliation," in *The Healing Circle: Essays in Cross-Cultural Mission* (Chicago, IL: CCGM Publications, 2000), 184–86.

13. Passover was a pilgrimage feast, when all Jews were required to assemble in Jerusalem for the celebration. News of the arrest, trial, and execution of Jesus would surely have spread quickly throughout the city.

were large-scale public events. We could think of this kind of listening to the story as "reading the signs of the times" and how events such as these affect people, especially those closest to those events and when the events are traumatic. The experience recounted in the Emmaus story is set in a much larger public context. In such cases, the story must be heard in that larger context. For the two disciples the important factors in such a story include (1) their shared experience, (2) which takes place within the context of the commonly known public events of that week in Jerusalem that had begun with a palm-waving welcome on Sunday and led to an incited mob crying for execution on Friday, (3) events that had drained away their hopes and fragile faith, (4) leaving them with unsatisfied hungers and (5) loss of resources to cope. We can flesh out this kind of listening more fully as we now look at some key threads connecting this walking with and listening to others with subsequent ministries, at how the pastoral dialogue continues.

Connecting the Ministries

The ministry of accompanying and listening flows into the next phase of the Emmaus story, ministry of the word, the focus in the next chapter.[14] If the ultimate goal of all the ministries is to help disciples of Jesus discover the meaning of their experience and discern what it means for their life of discipleship henceforth, it is essential to turn to the word of God when the time is appropriate.[15] It is there that the

14. Here and in each of the following chapters, making connections between the several forms of ministry will entail a certain amount of redundancy, as befits the reweaving. For that I beg the reader's indulgence and patience.

15. All pastoral ministers, each in their own way, incorporate elements of the word and its counsels for Christian living in what they do.

God story, the overarching story for a disciple's journey is to be found.

A key image, then, for making this first reweaving transition, from ministry of accompaniment to ministry of the word, is that of conversation between life story and biblical story.[16] Ministers of both companioning others and word have important questions to ask themselves.[17] For companioning ministry: how can the stories heard in pastoral companioning prepare for and contribute to the ministry of the word? For ministry of the word: how can the biblical story serve as a kind of catechetical and homiletic mystagogy for unraveling and naming the deeper meaning of life experiences? Ministry of the word is exercised preeminently in catechesis and homily.[18] That will require catechists and homilists to attend to the factors just named above, beginning with experience. Both of these forms of ministry of the word echo and break open the word for the gathered community.[19]

At this point, in anticipation of a fuller exploration in the next chapter, it is worth noting briefly that current catechetical theory, especially for the RCIA and adult faith formation, insists on the importance of attending to

16. A variation on this image of conversation from a mission perspective can be found in Stephen B. Bevans, "Mission as Prophetic Dialogue," the introduction to *Mission on the Road to Emmaus: Constants, Context and Prophetic Dialogue*, ed. Cathy Ross and Stephen B. Bevans (London: SCM Press, 2015), xi–xix.

17. Following the recommendation of Thomas H. Morris, "Liturgical Catechesis Revisited," *Catechumenate* 17, no. 3 (May 1994): 16, noted at the end of the previous chapter.

18. Other forms of ministry would include evangelization (e.g., Acts 2:14-42), retreat work, Bible study groups, group *lectio divina*, etc.

19. Though the word of God is rightly brought into play in pastoral ministry with individuals, the focus here is on ministry to the gathered community. That kind of ministry can also take place in written and other media, though the context is less personal and more open-ended.

experience.[20] This means also attending to the larger context in which people live; to their cultural, economic, and political context; to their human and religious needs; to the spiritual resources available to them; and to the issues they face in their way of life. Think of what the two disciples recounted of the experience that launched them on their journey to Emmaus, back to the life they had earlier left to follow Jesus. What had they sought in becoming his disciples? What were their hopes and hungers? How had these been left unfulfilled? And how spent were their resources now? Has their story of discipleship truly ended at this point in the narrative, or is it merely unfinished and on hold, waiting to be brought to a new birth of faith and hope in Christ? That is part of the intrigue and suspense of the Lukan narrative.

The starting point and goal are the same for homiletic ministry. It too is called to attend to the experience of the hearers, to the context in which they hear the word, to their understanding of what that word means for how they live.[21] It is to address "the needs of those to whom the church's preaching is directed, their culture and circumstances"; it should nurture their lives.[22] Homily preparation also begins

20. See, e.g., Congregation for the Clergy, *General Directory for Catechesis* 172, 174, https://www.vatican.va/roman_curia/congregations/cclergy/documents/rc_con_ccatheduc_doc_17041998_directory-for-catechesis_en.html; also International Council for Catechesis, *Adult Catechesis in the Christian Community: Some Principles and Guidelines* (Rome: Libreria Editrice Vaticana, St. Paul Publications, 1990), 56, http://www.vatican.va/roman_curia/congregations/cclergy/documents/rc_con_cclergy_doc_14041990_acat_en.html.

21. Bishops' Committee on Priestly Life and Ministry, *Fulfilled in Your Hearing: The Homily in the Sunday Assembly* (Washington, DC: USCCB, 1982), 4, 7, 10–14, https://www.usccb.org/beliefs-and-teachings/vocations/priesthood/priestly-life-and-ministry/upload/fiyh.pdf.

22. Congregation for Divine Worship and Discipline of the Sacraments, *Homiletic Directory* (Rome: Libreria Editrice Vaticana, 2015), 2, calls this

with walking with disciples and listening to the needs embedded in the stories they tell and to the context in which
that experience is situated.

Reweaving Strategies

Running through what has just been said about both catechesis and homily is the importance of listening for and
attending to the underlying stories. Both catechists and
homilists can benefit from conversing with colleagues in
the ministry of accompaniment. Again, following the strategy Thomas Morris recommends,[23] it would be good for
ministers of both pastoral companioning and word to ask
the questions of the other ministry, so that life stories and
the biblical story can be engaged in effective conversation.
Stories are not just accounts of isolated events. At their best
these stories sketch how things fit together and weave those
experiences into the longer story line of people's lives. It is
those life journeys that all ministers are to accompany and
that ministers of the word are to place within the founding
story common to the disciples of Jesus.[24]

So the practical strategic question is this: how can we
reweave the first phase of pastoral companioning with the
next phase of ministry of the word? The ministers of companioning need to ask anticipatory questions. What open-
ings are there in people's stories for fruitful conversation

---

one of four great Vatican II themes of importance for preaching, https://
www.vatican.va/roman_curia/congregations/ccdds/documents/rc
_con_ccdds_doc_20140629_direttorio-omiletico_en.html. See also GIRM
65.

23. Morris, "Liturgical Catechesis Revisited," 12–19, here at 16.

24. This is not an attempt to create a grand Christian master story (the
metanarrative much debated in postmodernism), but the more modest
effort to articulate a local community story fashioned in light of the biblical texts. Similarly, the four gospels can be seen as early Christians shaping the one gospel to meet local pastoral circumstances.

with biblical stories? How can the underlying common features of the stories of people's lives in this time and place be identified and brought into focus for the sake of the ministry of catechists and homilists to the community? We will focus here on the first side of making the connection, that is, listening to and gathering the shared stories people have to tell. The other side, how catechesis and homiletics make the connection from their side, will be explored more fully in the next chapter.[25]

The first step in the reweaving is looking for what is common in people's stories. The common thread may be obvious in cases of widespread loss and grief, such as the closing of parishes. It is much more difficult in more individual and personal reactions to change, such as major turnover in parish leadership. How might the underlying thread be identified then? What is envisioned here for companioning ministry is sifting through the stories of what people are experiencing to identify the common threads running through them. This means respecting their privacy and holding in utmost confidentiality the deeply personal details of their many stories. It means reflecting on those stories and finding the common contours and flows that lie within those experiences. It is analogous to looking at a family portrait. All the individuals in the family picture are unique, but one can also see general family resemblances among them. But the resemblances lie deeper than the surface events. My own experience tells me that the circumstances and events of my life are different from those of my siblings. But it doesn't take long listening to their stories to discover that the inner experience and feelings lying beneath and within their experiences are more alike than I would have expected. The first task of ministering to a com-

---

25. The strategies suggested here will apply to all the ministerial connections discussed in subsequent chapters and need not be repeated there.

munity is to discover how the experiences of people share such common underlying resemblances.

Second, gathering those stories and sifting out the common threads that bind them together is more than one pastor, or even a few members of the pastoral team, can easily accomplish. It is possible, however, with the aid of members of the various parish committees and ministries: for example, committees for peace and justice, for adult faith formation, for homily preparation, for care and visitation of the homebound, for bereavement, etc.—those who have their fingers on the pulse of community life in the particular local context. Also among those pulse-takers one should include perceptive parishioners who craft the weekly general intersessions for the Sunday liturgy and especially parish secretaries and all those who have their ear to the ground.[26] Perceptive practitioners in all the ministries, not just catechists and homilists, have windows of access to significant facets of the experience of the folks they serve. They can nuance and enrich the common threads that all the ministries gather for the weaving.

A collaborative effort works best for this. It starts with raising awareness that all ministers need to be alert to what is going on in the community, to ask the "what's happening?" and "tell me" questions. What stories do they hear? What struggles and issues do people commonly face in living as faith-filled disciples in the world around them? What are their hungers and hopes? How do they need to be cared for, nurtured, supported? What resources do they have or lack? And most important, as committee members gather these stories and sift through them, what are the common threads running through the experiences, the "family resemblances,"

---

26. Who listen not just for gossip and scuttlebutt but for the significant issues and questions people are facing.

which they can share with coworkers in pastoral ministry? What resonances are there with biblical stories?

Third, if this task is new to those who companion people in their various ministries, how can it be incorporated into their awareness and job descriptions? Through programs of professional preparation for catechists and homilists?[27] In briefings and resources for ongoing professional development in all the ministries? Through periodic parish staff development days that take time to do a serious reading of the local signs of the times and reflect on them? And how can they reflect together on the core inner meaning of what they are hearing? More on that in a moment.

Fourth, what opportunities are there for bringing these discoveries into an overarching collaboration among the ministries? Such opportunities can range from informal conversations in corridors and coffee rooms of parish centers to periodic full staff meetings that formally engage in this kind of reflection on a regular basis, especially at the beginning of liturgical seasons, at summer–school year intersections, and in the wake of major current events that affect people for good or ill.[28] Another way might be to have various ministry committees meet together on occasion (e.g., at the beginning of a season) to look at larger shared concerns, or to invite a representative from another committee to attend their meeting, or even to charge one of the regular committee members to gather information and report on what the other committees are hearing and to consistently voice the concerns, questions, and wisdom of those committees. Catechists and liturgists, for example, each need to hear and take account of each other's questions and what they are hearing from folks. Both need to hear the peace and justice questions.

27. *Adult Catechesis in the Christian Community*, 70–80; *Fulfilled in Your Hearing*, 43–44.
28. We'll return to these opportunities in chapter 7.

Fifth, how might pastoral ministers go about weaving the common threads that they have heard in people's stories into an appropriate coordination of the ministries that will work together to serve the members of their faith community on their life journey of discipleship? There is much wisdom to be gained from the growing theory and practice of what is commonly called theological reflection. Robert Kinast sums up the basic pattern that is common in the various approaches to such reflection. He describes it as a "deceptively simple threefold movement" consisting of (1) beginning with lived experience, (2) correlating that experience with Scripture and tradition, and (3) drawing practical implications for Christian living.[29] Christina Zaker, a faculty colleague with expertise in the use of theological reflection by pastoral ministers, has proposed using parables (stories), just as Jesus did, as a concrete way of doing this kind of reflection.[30] That meshes well with what has been said above about the central role shared story can play in reweaving the ministries. The lived experience told in that common story is seen afresh in the light of the Christian story and integrated into it for the sake of guiding how disciples are to live. For Zaker the goal of the reflection process is God-centered. That is clearly expressed in her definition: "Theological reflection at its best is a communal effort to discern God's presence in the world, to carve the space for that presence to invite us into a new vision, and to lay the groundwork for that new vision to take root in how we live our lives."[31]

---

29. Robert L. Kinast, *What Are They Saying about Theological Reflection?* (New York: Paulist Press, 2000), 1–5. In subsequent chapters Kinast briefly describes each of the major approaches to theological reflection.

30. Christina R. Zaker, "Parable as a Lens for Theological Reflection," *Reflective Practice: Formation and Supervision in Ministry* 35 (2015): 55–67.

31. Zaker, "Parable," 57–58. We will return to this reflective process in chapter 5 and appendix 2 on mystagogy.

This kind of process of collaborative reflection between the ministries deserves a prominent place in implementing a vision of a holistic approach to pastoral ministry. It is especially crucial for this first transition to get a rewoven vision of an integrated pastoral ministry off to a good start. It is the necessary bridge from ministry of pastoral companioning to ministries of the word on which the next chapter will focus.

The crucial implication behind these strategies for reweaving the ministries is that the community's leadership (pastor and staff, on whatever level of pastoral leadership) will have developed a vision of collaboration between the ministries and the commitment to implementing it.[32] This will require an effective practice of coordinating pastoral ministry to Christ's disciples through shared reflection on their journey. Such vision, commitment, and practice will invite ministers to think beyond the focused concerns and narrower boundaries of their own specialized ministries.[33] It challenges them to ask how they can all work together as coworkers, to accompany God's people on their lifelong journey of discipleship, and to mark the important moments

---

32. This would fit well within what the USCCB calls "parish culture." See *Our Hearts Were Burning within Us: A Pastoral Plan for Adult Faith Formation in the United States*, 122, https://www.usccb.org/beliefs-and-teachings/how-we-teach/catechesis/adult-faith-formation/our-hearts..

33. Kathleen A. Cahalan proposes that those called to a specialized role in ministry are to carry out their work in tandem with the other ministers, since they are all part of a ministerial community with responsibility to care for all aspects of ministry to disciples as disciples on their journey. See her "Toward a Fundamental Theology of Ministry," *Worship* 80, no. 2 (March 2006): 102–20, here at 119–20. An analogy might be doctors in general practice who have a working knowledge of many aspects of health care or, better, a team of doctors who coordinate their individual specialties in collaborative treatment of patients, each familiar with the pertinence of the others' specialties.

and stages of growth to which each of their ministries attend along the way.[34]

Summary Reflection

The goal for companioning is to listen to the experience of disciples or people seeking help, so that in ministry of the word we will then be able to help them discover not only that the Spirit of God is present and at work in their lives but also how Christ is walking with them and they with Christ on their journey.

---

34. For a detailed approach to forming coworkers for inter-ministry collaboration, see Jane E. Regan, *Where Two or Three Are Gathered: Transforming the Parish through Communities of Practice* (New York: Paulist Press, 2016), 27–46. She explores three constitutive elements important in forming a group for pastoral practice: shared experience, mutual engagements, and common repertoire (31–39).

3
Word

Emmaus Story

> [25]Then he said to them, "Oh, how foolish you are, and how slow of heart to believe all that the prophets have declared! [26]Was it not necessary that the Messiah should suffer these things and then enter into his glory?" [27]Then beginning with Moses and all the prophets, he interpreted to them the things about himself in all the scriptures.

Paradigm for Ministry

At the gentle invitation of the stranger who has joined them on the road, walking with them and listening so well, the truth of their experience has now been told, and it has been heard by the stranger with empathy and respect. Their story had ended with their downhearted admission, "we had hoped" (Luke 24:21). It had ended in failure. That pained admission of disillusionment and lost hope immediately leads into the next scene in Luke's narrative.

When the two have exhausted their story, the stranger replies: "Oh, how foolish you are, and how slow of heart to believe all that the prophets have declared!" (v. 25). He immediately tells them that the ending of the story is very different. His version ends, not in failure, but in triumph, in glory: "Was it not necessary that the Messiah should suffer these things and then enter into his glory?" (v. 26). He

35

then proceeds to retell the very same story, "beginning with
Moses and all the prophets" (v. 27).

There is a sheer mastery in the stranger's retelling of their
story. The experience that has been recounted is theirs. The
words of the retelling are also theirs, familiar words recalled
from Moses and all the prophets. But what is new is how
those familiar words are now broken open to take on an
unforeseen meaning: "he interpreted to them the things
about himself in all the scriptures" (v. 27). Those familiar
words now bear and name in a new way not only the past
experience of their people but what they themselves had
just experienced. That is biblical "interpreting" (v. 27) or
"opening up" (v. 32) the Scriptures at its best. Though they
would only put it into words later, when they could name
the "burning of their hearts" (v. 32), the impact of such storytelling is predictable, as is also its sequel, as we shall see
in the next chapter.

The stranger's response to the experience of the two disciples models a fundamental strategy for all ministry of the
word, especially catechesis[1] and homiletics. It rests on relating experience and the word of God and bringing them into
dialogue with each other—the story of human experience
taken up into the story told in God's word and given new
meaning there. Jesus put it succinctly in his first public appearance in his hometown synagogue in Nazareth, as recorded by Luke. After reading the passage from Isaiah
61:1-2, Jesus rolled up the scroll, handed it to the attendant,
sat down, and said, "Today this scripture has been fulfilled
in your hearing" (Luke 4:21).

That strategy of correlating human experience and God's
word runs throughout the ministry of Jesus. Think of how
often he uses the everyday experience of his hearers to

---

1. For more on catechesis, see the technical note in appendix 1 of this
book.

frame his message about the reign of God and how God wishes people to live within it. There are parables, folk sayings, and current events. For example, he speaks about sowing seed (Matt 13:18), choosing safe foundations on which to build a house (Matt 7:24-27), practices of hiring and paying day laborers (Matt 20:1-16), reading the signs of the weather (Matt 16:1-3), catching fish (Luke 5:4), hearing news about a tower that collapsed and killed eighteen people (Luke 13:4), and having his feet washed (Luke 7:36-50). In the words of Jesus such experiences from daily life provide an opportunity to convey an insight about life within the reign of God, what God has in mind for us. Think also of what Jesus inculcated in his Sermon on the Mount (Matt 5:1–7:29), the sermon on the plain (Luke 6:17-49), and his other discourses. A variety of lessons for life in God's reign can be drawn from these passages and so many more.

This poses a question for ministers of companioning and word. Are they companioning disciples who have lost their way and need to recover their Jesus story, like the two on the road to Emmaus? Or other potential disciples who need to discover for the first time a Jesus story to clarify their way? What connections with the gospel message of Jesus are we to listen for in the lives of people? Are there dominant threads among the values and behaviors that run through all these teachings of Jesus and his way of acting toward others? Or in a more comprehensive way, one might find an applicable theme in his answer to the lawyer's question (Matt 22:34-40; also Mark 12:30-31; Luke 10:27): " 'You shall love the Lord your God with all your heart, and with all your soul, and with all your mind.' This is the greatest and first commandment. And the second is like it: 'You shall love your neighbor as yourself.' On these two commandments hang all the law and the prophets." Love is the wellspring of so many of the values and behaviors that should mark the lives of those who would follow or could follow

Jesus: inclusion and acceptance of others, help and healing for them, self-giving service of neighbor, forgiveness of offenses, mercy, love of enemies, and more. Jesus taught and modeled all of these, ultimately giving the total gift of self; there is "no . . . greater love than this" (John 15:13). Pope Francis has written: "The heart of [the Gospel's] message will always be the same: the God who revealed his immense love in the crucified and risen Christ."[2] That is the journey into the "mystery of Christ"[3] into which all pastoral ministers invite others to enter as they listen to their experience and bring it into conversation with the Gospel. That strategy is especially important for catechetical and homiletic ministry today.

Connecting the Ministries

Making the connection will entail starting from experience and putting it into conversation with the word.

Starting from Experience

In the previous chapter we noted that both catechesis and homiletics start from experience. How can they each find a generative theme to focus on from experience? A first, more generic resource for both catechesis and homiletics to draw on would be the collaborative "reading" of the current context by a coordinated approach to a ministry of companioning recommended in the previous chapter. Catechetical and homiletic ministry each have a more narrowly focused resource of their own to name the starting experience. That focus for catechesis is often determined by an overall program of topics, and the weekly focus for preaching is nor-

2. *Evangelii Gaudium* 11, http://www.vatican.va/content/francesco/en/apost_exhortations/documents/papa-francesco_esortazione-ap_20131124_evangelii-gaudium.html.

3. *Catechesi Tradendae* 5; see also Eph 3:9, 18-19; 1 John 4:7-12.

mally dependent on the assigned biblical passages. Even in those cases, however, development of some aspect of the theme or passage can be seen to address the present context, and experience remains a central concern for connecting our human stories and the biblical story.

Current catechetical theory makes two demands regarding participants' experience. Catechesis must acknowledge and take into account what people have experienced in their lives; it also requires that people experience catechetical formation itself as something in which they participate actively and fully. Catechesis is to affirm and draw on the wisdom participants have gained from their experience and engage them in conversations and discernment about things that matter to their lives. In a word, catechetical ministry begins with listening to and taking account of the experience of the participants. First, their experience of life as disciples is to be put in dialogue with the way of discipleship proposed in Scripture, echoed in tradition, and brought to bear for their lives in catechesis (echoing is the literal meaning of "catechesis"), and, second, they are to be active participants in that dialogue.[4]

---

4. Among the official Roman Catholic documents, see *General Directory for Catechesis* 152–53, 157, 172–74, https://www.vatican.va/roman_curia/ congregations/cclergy/documents/rc_con_ccatheduc_doc_17041998 _directory-for-catechesis_en.html; International Council for Catechesis, *Adult Catechesis in the Christian Community: Some Principles and Guidelines* (Rome: Libreria Editrice Vaticana, St. Paul Publications, 1990), especially 54–58, http://www.vatican.va/roman_curia/congregations/cclergy /documents/rc_con_cclergy_doc_14041990_acat_en.html; and NCCB, *Our Hearts Were Burning within Us* 64–66, 82, https://www.usccb.org /beliefs-and-teachings/how-we-teach/catechesis/adult-faith-formation /our-hearts. Among prominent catechetical theorists, see Thomas H. Groome, *Will There Be Faith? A New Vision for Educating and Growing Disciples* (New York: HarperOne, 2011), esp. chapters 8–9; Jane E. Regan, *Toward an Adult Church: A Vision of Faith Formation* (Chicago, IL: Loyola Press, 2002), esp. 162–64.

The same strategy has been proposed for homiletic ministry. It too is called to attend to the experience of the hearers, to the context in which they hear the word, and to their understanding of what that word means for how they live.[5] In order to nurture their lives, it should address "the needs of those to whom the Church's preaching is directed, their culture and circumstances."[6] Homily preparation also begins in walking with disciples and listening to the needs and hungers embedded in the stories they tell and to the context in which that experience is situated. This listening can be done in person and especially with the assistance of others.[7] Again, homily preparation is to be attentive as well to the context in which that experience happened. Karl Barth has famously said that the preacher needs to have the Bible in one hand and the daily newspaper in the other.

A true story illustrates well the wisdom of making this connection. It took place in April 1970. A pastor asked a rabbi friend, who was famous for his preaching, to attend Sunday Mass and give him some feedback. After the celebration, the pastor waited with great anticipation for what his friend would have to say. The rabbi remained silent. When the pastor asked why, the rabbi's only reply was simple: "Don't you know what happened this week?" What had happened that week was the explosion on board Apollo 13, later retold

5. Bishops' Committee on Priestly Life and Ministry, *Fulfilled in Your Hearing: The Homily in the Sunday Assembly* (Washington, DC: USCCB, 1982), 4, 7, 10–14, https://www.usccb.org/beliefs-and-teachings/vocations /priesthood/priestly-life-and-ministry/upload/fiyh.pdf.

6. Congregation for Divine Worship and Discipline of the Sacraments, *Homiletic Directory* (Rome: Libreria Editrice Vaticana, 2015), 2, calls this one of four great Vatican II themes of importance for preaching, online at: https://www.vatican.va/roman_curia/congregations/ccdds/documents /rc_con_ccdds_doc_20140629_direttorio-omiletico_en.html. See also GIRM 65.

7. An effective way to accomplish this collaborative listening is through what the bishops of this country call a "Homily Preparation Group." See *Fulfilled in Your Hearing*, 36–38.

dramatically in a riveting movie. People were horrified that the astronauts were in danger of being marooned in space forever. The rabbi continued: "That is what is on the minds and hearts of your people today, and you never mentioned it even once. There is nothing I can say to you."

The preacher's goal is to help listeners to hear the story of their own experience told again within the biblical story, that is, the story of Jesus, which is to be a Christian's master story.[8] Only thus can the preacher meet the homiletic ideal voiced by Jesus to the people in his hometown synagogue after he had proclaimed the passage from the prophet Isaiah: "Today this scripture has been fulfilled in your hearing" (Luke 4:21). In those few words the passage from Isaiah is broken open to reveal that the story of God's ancient promise to them would come to fulfillment through Jesus and that they were to be part of it.

Running through what has just been said about both catechesis and homiletics is the importance of listening for and attending to both the underlying stories people bring and the story told in the Scriptures about how God desires people to live.[9] Among all the stories out of which we each live, one typically becomes the central story. For disciples,

---

8. "Master story" is not meant here as the "grand narrative" critiqued in postmodern thought, a "metanarrative" globalizing all other stories. It is used more modestly here, as a particular way of remembering and telling a story to make sense in a particular local context. In this vein, Edward Schillebeeckx once said in a lecture that we do not have "*the* gospel," only four gospels that tell that gospel story in the local context of a particular community to meet their particular pastoral needs. That is what each community needs to do, without displacing the authority of the original four gospels, the only ones from our founding days. On narrative approach to Scripture, see Leland Ryken, *How Bible Stories Work: A Guided Study of Biblical Narrative* (Bellingham, WA: Lexham Press, 2018).

9. Regarding preaching, see Herbert Anderson, "Narrative Preaching and Narrative Reciprocity," in *A Handbook for Catholic Preaching*, ed. Edward Foley (Collegeville, MN: Liturgical Press, 2016), 169–79.

that central story is to be the Jesus story. Stories are not just accounts of isolated events. As noted earlier, at their best stories sketch how things fit together and weave those experiences into the longer story line of disciples' lives journeying with the God who came to live among us.[10] It is those life journeys that ministers of the word are to put into conversation with the word of God. For both catechesis and the homily are to echo and proclaim the person of Jesus and the way of life he taught.[11]

Conversing with the Word

A number of years ago James Dunning, long-time director of the North American Forum on the Catechumenate, wrote that "if the authors of scripture are more homilists than historians, what we said earlier of homilists is true of them. They do not preach a message *at* us. They enter into conversation *with* us."[12] Dunning then recommends an approach in which

---

10. The Greek verb *eskēnōsen* means literally that the Word of God pitched a tent among us and lived in it.

11. "The primary and essential object of catechesis . . . is 'the mystery of Christ.' . . . The definitive aim of catechesis is to put people not only in touch but in communion, in intimacy, with Jesus Christ: only he can lead us to the love of the Father in and make us share in the life of the Holy Trinity" (*Catechesi Tradendae* 5; also in CCC 426). The homily is "a proclamation of God's wonderful works in the history of salvation, the mystery of Christ, ever present and active within us" (see SC 35.2; also *Homiletic Directory* 10).

12. James B. Dunning, *Echoing God's Word: Formation for Catechists and Homilists in a Catechumenal Church* (Arlington, VA: The North American Forum on the Catechumenate, 1993), 166. See also Pope Francis, *Evangelii Gaudium* (2013), 137–44, where the themes of conversation and dialogue are threaded throughout the pope's reflections on the liturgical homily; http://www.vatican.va/content/francesco/en/apost_exhortations /documents/papa-francesco_esortazione-ap_20131124_evangelii -gaudium.html.

hearing the story will be the first task of a pastoral/theo-
logical hearing of scripture—to move through the story
world of the text to understand the plot, setting, conflicts,
questions and characters and to see what light they shed
on our plot, setting, conflicts, questions and characters.
In that way, when we form our theology, we will seek not
just historical facts and not just the psychological inner
states and feelings of the characters but also a pastoral
understanding that cares for and liberates people in practical ways.[13]

In a subsequent chapter Dunning outlines these four
movements in such a shared pastoral/theological process
of "conversing with scripture":

- *Initial Understandings*
  [proclamation of the text several times, silent reflection,
  sharing of immediate reactions: impressions, words/
  phrases, feelings, mood; an unaided reading that reveals
  participants' personal world "out front" (180–81)]

- *Listening to the Text on Its Own Grounds*
  [an aided reading with help of resources / resource person, which reveals the "world of the text" and "world
  behind the text"; more an act of worship than a quest for
  knowledge, guided by one who can lead us toward any
  pastoral "so whats" in order "to offer us a vision, a
  method and an access to the world and story of the gospel
  authors so that ministers of the word can help homilists
  and catechists enter into conversation with God's word"
  (181–82)]

- *Getting the Meaning "Out in Front"*
  ["after hearing the text on its own ground . . . move to
  the claims it makes on today and tomorrow in our relationships with contemporary (situations). We first get to

---

13. Dunning, *Echoing God's Word*, 167.

the meaning 'behind the text' to get 'out in front' of the
text. We go beyond the intention of the first speaker and
the attention of the first hearer. We converse with the
word in our world" (182–83), the shared world out front]

- *Sharing Our New Response*
  [then, with the help of a facilitator, "we share our new
  response . . . in concrete, practical ways that challenge
  our lives, families, churches and neighborhoods, and our
  civic, national and world communities" (183–84)][14]

Dunning offers this way of conversing with Scripture for the
formation and ministerial work of both catechists and homilists. Experienced practitioners will surely be able to adjust
this general approach to their own skills and contexts.

How to connect ministry of word to the companioning
question has been our main focus in this chapter. How can
catechesis and homiletics build on what pastoral companions have learned about the possibilities of opening up
people's experience to the gospel message? Or to put the
question from the reverse angle, how can they open up the
gospel message to embrace people's experience? That is the
question ministers of both companioning and word should
be asking.

Before taking up the particulars of reweaving strategies,
we should pause to note Morris's recommendation to ask
the liturgical question as well. Anticipation of the liturgy
question will be important for preparatory liturgical catechesis. It will be especially important for homilists, since
their ministry flows over beyond the time of preparation
into the liturgy itself. What moments of witnessing to the
gospel values in their daily lives can people bring to the liturgy to be opened up in the homily? What experience of

14. Dunning, *Echoing God's Word*, 176–84; the headings, with abbrevi-
ated summaries inserted in brackets.

self-giving and rising to new ways of acting can people bring to be offered as their spiritual sacrifice along with Christ?

Reweaving Strategies

We turn now to particular strategies for bringing life stories and the biblical story into conversation and reweaving these ministries. The human story heard must become a story retold in a new way; experience must be broken open and renamed. How can that movement from the stories heard by pastoral companions to ministry of the word be facilitated in catechesis and homiletics?

In Catechesis

One such strategy is illustrated in the interactive reflective catechetical approach advocated by Thomas Groome. In his most recent book, he names this approach bringing "life to Faith to life."[15] Using the example of Jesus, seen most clearly in the Emmaus story, Groome identifies the following movements in this approach:

- Beginning with people's lives,

- Encouraging their own reflections,

- Teaching them [Jesus'] gospel with authority,

- Inviting them to see for themselves, to take his teaching to heart, and

- Encouraging their decisions for lived faith as disciples.[16]

---

15. Thomas H. Groome, *Will There Be Faith?* For a full explanation of this approach, see chapters 8 and 9. Groome first formulated this approach in the late 1970s and has continued to develop it in articles and two previous books.

16. Groome, *Will There Be Faith?*, 29–38, here at 34 (formatting original).

The first two and last two movements are participant-centered; the middle movement is facilitator-centered. Groome's underlying premise is that both present experience (movements one and two) and the inherited tradition (movement three) are sources of wisdom and that engaging participants in dialogue between those two sources of wisdom can effectively lead them to deepening growth in their future lived experience (movements four and five).[17]

In an approach to catechetical ministry such as Groome's, the bridge from experience to word is established in the preliminary stages of catechesis, that is, in the choice of and entry into the focal theme to be explored and reflected on. That involves identifying what Groome calls the "generative theme."[18] This is a theme that is of real interest to people and meaningful to their lives, one that is apt to lead them into full and active engagement. The theme can be drawn from life's experiences or from the life of faith. In the case of the two disciples on the way, the stranger draws out the theme latent in their experience by asking those simple two questions: "what are you discussing?" and "what things?" (Luke 24:17, 19). The generative theme that spilled out from the two disciples' dejected account of their experience was the loss of all the hope they had placed in Jesus and his mission (v. 21). The stranger also names it as a loss of faith in him and his mission (v. 25). The generative theme thus finds expression in two words: hope and faith.

In Groome's approach, the generative theme is then given expression, whether in word, symbol, or ritual, in what he

17. For a similar process, see Anne Marie Mongoven, *The Prophetic Spirit of Catechesis: How We Share the Fire in Our Hearts* (New York: Paulist Press, 2000), 120–41 on the process of "symbolic catechesis"; and Regan, *Toward an Adult Church*, 87–95 on the "transformative learning" process.

18. See Groome, *Will There Be Faith?*, 286–89.

describes as the "focusing act"[19] that introduces the cate-chetical session or a series of sessions. The intent of the focusing act is to

(1) engage participants with the generative theme,

(2) lend them a shared sense of the reflection to follow, and

(3) draw them into active conversation around what that theme means in their lives.[20]

This focusing act opens up a bridge from experience into catechesis.

In Homiletics

In preaching ministry the identification of the homiletic theme usually starts from a reading of the assigned Scripture passages, especially the gospel. Occasionally it can also start from an issue or prevailing mood being widely experienced at that time. In either case, to ensure that the theme chosen accurately addresses what people need to hear, *Fulfilled in Your Hearing* notes that "an effective way for preachers to be sure that they are addressing some of the real concerns of the congregation in the homily is to involve members of that congregation in a homily preparation group."[21] The document goes on to say that such a group, small but with periodic rotation of members who are representative of the community to keep it fresh, can be helpful in raising the issues of concern to the people and be a rich resource of insight into God's presence in people's lives.

---

19. See Groome, *Will There Be Faith?*, 304–9.
20. Groome, *Will There Be Faith?*, 304, paraphrased.
21. *Fulfilled in Your Hearing*, 36.

Fulfilled in Your Hearing then outlines a method a homily preparation group can follow. It consists of these seven steps:

– read the passages,

– share the words,

– exegete the texts,

– share the good news,

– share the challenge these words offer us,

– explore the consequences, and

– give thanks and praise.[22]

The steps in this approach to homily preparation are an expanded version of the traditional way of praying with Scripture known as *lectio divina* (holy reading). A subsequent document from Rome, the *Homily Directory*, also notes that "the dynamic of *lectio divina* offers a fruitful paradigm for an understanding of the role of the homily in the liturgy and how this affects the process of preparation."[23] To the traditional four steps (*lectio, meditatio, oratio,* and *contemplatio*) the *Directory* adds a fifth step, *actio*.

This kind of approach to preparing the Sunday homily has been used both in parishes and in ecumenical associations of local pastors. A family mass group within a parish where I frequently preside has used an adapted version of the homily preparation group proposed by *Fulfilled in Your Hearing* for several decades. Planning the Sunday celebra-

22. *Fulfilled in Your Hearing*, 36–38 subtitles.

23. Congregation for Divine Worship and Discipline of the Sacraments, *Homiletic Directory*, 26–36, https://www.vatican.va/roman_curia /congregations/ccdds/documents/rc_con_ccdds_doc_20140629 _direttorio-omiletico_en.html.

tion two weeks in advance, the group spends the first hour in *lectio divina*. That portion of the evening concludes with a reflective naming of how the readings both affirm and challenge the community in its context and way of life. This experience has proven to be of immense value to presiders in preparing a homily in which the word proclaimed can speak of and to their lives. Only then does the group go on to the detailed planning of the celebration in a way that is coherent with what the *lectio* has revealed to them.

Up to this point we have explored a first connective task: how ministry of the word links back to the stories of experience uncovered in a ministry of companioning disciples that has gone before. It should be noted that each of the catechetical and homiletic strategies described above also move in the other direction. The final step(s) in each of the next ministries also looks forward to what the conversation between life story and biblical story will mean for the life of disciples henceforth. That conversation continues in a privileged way when disciples gather together around word and table, bringing to these ritual centers the silent proclamation of lived witness and the spiritual worship of their living sacrifice to the table. That is how they link their life to liturgy and liturgy to their life beyond the gathering. To that table ministry we will turn in the next chapter.

Summary Reflection

The main goal of ministry of the word is to help disciples learn to retell the story of their lives in terms of the gospel story. That is how they will be able to name the presence and working of God's Spirit in their lives and how Christ is walking with them and they with Christ on a journey to newness of life.

4
Table

Emmaus Story

[28]As they came near the village to which they were going, he walked ahead as if he were going on. [29]But they urged him strongly, saying, "Stay with us, because it is almost evening and the day is now nearly over." So he went in to stay with them. [30]When he was at the table with them, he took bread, blessed and broke it, and gave it to them. [31]Then their eyes were opened, and they recognized him; and he vanished from their sight.

Paradigm for Ministry

In keeping with the flow of the Emmaus account, this chapter will reflect on how a new biblical retelling of life stories as silent proclamation and living sacrifice can then be woven into the ministry of liturgy that follows. How can they be linked together?

The Lukan account links them in a dialogue of hospitality. At the stranger's invitation the two disciples had told their story. In response he has accepted with reverence their version of the story and has given that same story back to them to retell, but with a new ending. Although they cannot yet name what they are experiencing, their hearts have been set on fire by that new way of telling the story. The stranger who companioned them on the way has given them a double gift. He has hosted their hurts and restored their hopes. The hospitality he extended to them evokes their offer of hospitality in return,[1] a grateful invitation to share their table: "Stay with us, because it is almost evening and the day is now nearly over. So he went in to stay with them"[2] (Luke 24:29).

Note, first, that the stranger does not force their invitation. He acts as though he is going on and simply awaits their offer of hospitality. The movement from ministry of word to ministry of table cannot be forced; it can only be freely offered and accepted when the time is right. In the Emmaus story the transition from word to table is clearly sequential, and the disciples' response of hospitality to the gift of hospitality the stranger had offered them is the link. In the prior ministry of Jesus the movement from word to table is often less clearly demarcated; word and table often coincide. A word, then, about the table practice of Jesus.

The Gospel of Luke, more than any other, is filled with stories of Jesus at table. His table practice is indiscriminate,[3] to the consternation of the scandalized Pharisees and scribes. "This fellow welcomes sinners and eats with them," they grumbled (Luke 15:2, also 5:30). How can he possibly be of God if he acts like that? Note too that some of the meal scenes of Jesus typically present him as confronting the ways of his table companions whose behaviors are inimical to how people are to live in God's reign. Their experience is brought into the open and challenged. Think of the meal

1. For a reflection on the thread of hospitality woven through the final part of the Emmaus story, see Michael Kwatera, "We Have Seen the Lord," *Liturgical Ministry* 3 (Winter 1994): 31–34.

2. This moment is beautifully captured in the bas-relief in the pilgrims' cloister ambulatory in Santo Domingo de Silos in Spain. It shows the stranger doing a crossover dance step in response to their invitation to stay.

3. The inclusivity shown so prominently in his meal practice is characteristic of the ministry of Jesus, as noted earlier in chapter 1.

Table 53

with Levi, called to leave tax collecting to follow Jesus (5:27-39); or the Pharisees and scholars of the law who place ritual observance above concern for neighbor and love of God (11:37-54); or the Pharisees who invite wealthy guests to positions of honor at table and neglect to include those who are poor, crippled, lame, blind (14:7-24). Jesus challenges his table companions to conversion, reconciliation, inclusion, service of others. In other meal scenes, such as the meal at the home of Mary and Martha (10:38-42) and the Last Supper (22:24-30), Jesus teaches receptive followers about life in the reign of God. In both kinds of table scenes, the table practice of Jesus embodies the values of God's reign, shared in word and food.

What do these meal stories have to do with liturgy, with Eucharist? A first clue can be found in the account of the feeding of the multitudes (Luke 9:10-17). After teaching the crowds about the reign of God, Jesus hosted them at an unexpected feast on five loaves and two fish. "Taking the five loaves and the two fish, he looked up to heaven, and blessed and broke them, and gave them to the disciples to set before the crowd" (9:16). The words "take / bless / break / give," already well known to Luke's audience from decades of celebrating the Lord's Supper, would have carried eucharistic overtones for them.[4]

To take this a step further, a masterful study of the meal practice of Jesus in Luke's gospel by Scripture scholar Eugene LaVerdiere helps us connect word and table.[5] He

---

4. This formula occurs in all six accounts of this event (Matt 14:13-21; 15:32-38; Mark 6:34-44; 8:1-9; Luke 9:19-17; and John 6:1-14), twice the number of the synoptic Last Supper accounts with these words.

5. Eugene LaVerdiere, *Dining in the Kingdom of God: The Origins of the Eucharist according to Luke* (Chicago, IL: Liturgy Training Publications, 1994). LaVerdiere's focus is different from ours. He is studying the series of these meals to decipher in them the origins of the Eucharist, rather than isolate a single event of "institution" (3–5). For him the Last Supper is part of that entire meal practice of Jesus, but it is also a key moment

focuses on Luke's accounts of ten meals of Jesus.[6] Eight of them take place during his earthly ministry, and three of them after that. LaVerdiere counts the Last Supper as belonging to both sets. It is Jesus' last earthly supper, but it also inaugurates the coming reign of God: "I tell you, I will not eat it [the Passover meal] until it is fulfilled in the kingdom of God. . . . I tell you that from now on I will not drink of the fruit of the vine until the kingdom of God comes" (Luke 22:16, 18). It is only then that Jesus takes and blesses the bread before the actual meal and the cup of wine after it (22:19-20), the meal now taking place within the kingdom. The Last Supper links the other meals into a continuing meal practice and brings the latent eucharistic overtones of the entire meal practice of Jesus to their fullest expression. That fully eucharistic meaning carries over immediately into the next of those ten meals, the supper at Emmaus, the first celebration of Eucharist in the post-resurrection community led by the risen Lord in person. As such, the supper at Emmaus deserves to be honored as the paradigm for all subsequent celebrations of the Eucharist.

Several key theological reflections can help to draw out how central the Emmaus scene is for our reweaving of the ministries. First, the entire pattern of the Emmaus narrative is condensed in the Eucharist as we now know it. The Lord gathers with the disciples on the way and then again at the table, as we do when we gather for Eucharist. The Scriptures are proclaimed and broken open on the way, as we do in the Liturgy of the Word. Bread is blessed, broken, and shared (and

---

within it. Together these meals could each unveil thematic nuances for the meaning of the Eucharist, and they indeed serve as "*a compendium of the whole gospel*" (2, emphasis original).

6. Luke 5:27-39; 7:36-50; 9:10-17; 10:38-42; 11:37-54; 14:1-24; 19:1-10; 27:7-38; 24:13-35, 36-53. For a fuller survey of the theme of food in Luke, see Robert J. Karris, *Eating Your Way through Luke's Gospel* (Collegeville, MN: Liturgical Press, 2006).

Table 55

wine is blessed, poured, and shared), as we do in the Liturgy of the Eucharist. Finally, having recognized the risen Lord at table and with hearts set afire by his words, the disciples are empowered to return with a mission to tell the others "how he had been made known to them in the breaking of the bread" (Luke 24:35), just as we too are nourished by him and sent forth in the concluding rite from Eucharist on mission to the world to spread the good news. The pattern of Jesus' life and ministry summed up in the Emmaus narrative is also the larger pattern for our ministries, brought into focus every time we gather to celebrate the Lord's Supper.

Second, reflecting on the table scene verse by verse can lead us to the deeper meaning this paradigmatic pattern can have. Though the two disciples had initiated the table scene by inviting the stranger to stay with them, when they are at table the stranger assumes the role of leading them in the meal prayer over the bread (v. 30). The guest becomes the host, completing a second round of the dialogue of hospitality in the Emmaus account. He had ministered to them on the way; now he ministers as their risen *leitourgos* (liturgist), if we may borrow that word from Hebrews (8:2). That has been true at our Eucharists ever since. The risen Lord remains our *leitourgos*, and the whole assembly becomes *leitourgos* with him (CCC 1187–88).

Third, "when he was at table with them, he took bread, blessed and broke it, and gave it to them" (Luke 24:30). These words are cryptic in the Emmaus account, without any further detail. In their catechesis and liturgies over several decades, early Christians had already become familiar with the formulaic version of the eucharistic words in the Emmaus account.[7] To the typical Jewish table actions and blessing prayers over bread and wine at the Last Supper,

---

7. The earliest written eucharistic account we have of these words is in 1 Corinthians 11:23-25 (usually dated between 53 and 55 CE). They are also found in the six gospel accounts of the feeding of the multitudes.

Jesus added words giving the bread and wine a new meaning: "This [loaf of bread] is my body, which is given for you. . . . This cup that is poured out for you is the new covenant in my blood" (Luke 22:19-20). In these words Jesus names the meaning his death on the morrow will have. His death is not to be merely an end to his life of ministry but rather the final culminating act of that ministry, the total offering of his life for others. That offering has passed over into an eternal phase, for "he is able for all time to save those who approach God through him, since he always lives to make intercession for them" (Heb 7:25). And so it is, even now. That timeless giving over of himself into the hands of God to intercede for us is always present in our every eucharistic "now." We will return in a moment to the other words Jesus added at the Last Supper.

Fourth, when the stranger had joined them on the way, "their eyes were kept from recognizing him" (Luke 24:16). But now, in the "breaking of the bread" at the table, "their eyes were opened, and they recognized him" (v. 31). In the appearance accounts, it should be noted, recognition of the risen Jesus is never simply a physical recognition that the Jesus of Nazareth whom they had known is still alive. Rather, the one who shares the meal with the disciples is recognized in faith, not simply as the earthly Jesus of Nazareth, but as "the Lord" (John 21:7). That moment of recognition is not mere physical sight but "faith insight."[8] In the breaking of the bread the two disciples come to know that the stranger is the Lord, risen and now with them. Their sad story of the life and ministry of Jesus had ended with his death (Luke 24:19-24). They did not yet have the final part of the kerygma of the early church, the story of his resurrection. Their hearts had been filled with inner dark-

---

8. See Raymond E. Brown, *The Virginal Conception and Bodily Resurrection of Jesus* (New York: Paulist Press, 1973), 111–14.

Table 57

ness as they left Emmaus in the full light of day. Now, in the dusk of that evening, the full light of Easter faith has dawned in their hearts.

When the disciples' eyes are opened in recognition, they also recognize something about themselves. Their original story is told in the past tense: "we had hoped that he was the one to redeem Israel" (v. 21). Their discipleship and any further involvement in the mission of Jesus are over. Now, however, in recognizing that Jesus is alive, they also recognize who they still are; their faith and hope are reborn. They are still his disciples[9] and indeed "missionary disciples,"[10] for the mission he gave them while on earth still holds as well.

Fifth, to those words of interpretation he added to the prayers over the bread and cup at the Last Supper, Jesus had also made another addition. He commanded: "Do this in remembrance of me" (Luke 22:19). This command is not only a rubrical instruction to celebrate the table rite as his memorial; it also presents a larger challenge for them. What is the larger "this" his disciples are to do? Is it not the same "this" that Jesus is doing?[11] As noted above, his words over

9. Perhaps in that moment of the breaking and giving of the bread the two disciples suddenly remembered that happening at table with Jesus three evenings earlier and their ignominious flight in the garden afterward (Mark 14:50). Perhaps in that moment of flashback they now understood that Jesus was at this Emmaus table, and in giving them the broken bread again he was restoring them to discipleship.

10. A phrase used by Pope Francis in *Evangelii Gaudium* (2013), 120, http://www.vatican.va/content/francesco/en/apost_exhortations /documents/papa-francesco_esortazione-ap_20131124_evangelii -gaudium.html.

11. The "this" (*touto* in Greek), which is neuter, refers not to the bread (árton), which is masculine, but rather to the entirety of Christ's action, to the Eucharist as a whole. See Xavier Léon Dufour, *Sharing the Eucharistic Bread: The Witness of the New Testament*, trans. Matthew J. O'Connell (New York: Paulist Press, 1987), 109–10, and Léon Dufour, "Do This in Memory of Me," *Theology Digest* 36, no. 1 (Spring 1978): 36–39.

the bread and cup interpret in advance the meaning of what he is to do on the morrow. They assign to his death on the cross the meaning of total redemptive self-giving in love.[12] His disciples are to do likewise, to make a complete offering of their lives in loving service of others, in memory of and along with him.[13]

In sum this is the gift of self we bring to the eucharistic gathering, symbolized by the cross, candles, and book in the entrance procession. This is the gift of ourselves we place on the altar when the gifts of bread and wine are presented; the prayers over the bread and wine speak of them as multifaceted gifts—of God, earth, and human work—indeed the gift of all that we do and are. And then we pray for the transformation of bread and wine into Christ given for us and of ourselves as a living sacrifice given for others. It is to continue that gift of self to others that we are then sent.

Connecting the Ministries

Those reflections set the stage for a deeper understanding of how eucharistic table ministry helps us make connections, both to the ministries of companioning and word that have gone before and to those of mystagogy and mission that will follow.

Building on Companioning and Word

In the two previous chapters, we have seen that the purpose of the ministry of companioning is to listen to the stories of

---

12. Some scholars also speak of the words interpreting the bread and wine as an enacted prophecy. In them his final self-gift is already made.

13. See Gilbert Ostdiek, "We Offer You This Holy and Living Sacrifice," *New Theology Review* 19, no. 2 (May 2006): 81–83; "Eucaristía / Memorial de la Pasión," in *Pasión de Jesucristo*, Diccionarios San Pablo, ed. Luis Díez Merino, Robin Ryan, Adolfo Lippi (Madrid: San Pablo, 2015), 439–49.

Table 59

peoples' lives, attending to what shapes their experience and their days. The ministry of the word, especially catechetical and homiletic breaking open of the word, then places those stories in conversation with the gospel story, so that people can find in it a deeper understanding of the meaning and purpose of their lives, namely, to give oneself in loving service of others as Jesus did and to offer that gift of self with him. That is the goal of their life journey and spiritual path as missionary disciples.

The Constitution on the Sacred Liturgy (*Sacrosanctum Concilium*) establishes an unequivocal norm: "In the reform and promotion of the liturgy, this full and active participation by all the people [their right and duty by reason of their baptism] is *the aim to be considered by all else*" (SC 14, emphasis added). In the Dogmatic Constitution on the Church (*Lumen Gentium*), Vatican II calls the Eucharist the "source and summit of the christian life," for in it Christians "offer the divine victim to God and themselves along with him" (LG 11). The General Instruction of the Roman Missal offers a healthy reminder for the presider and liturgical ministers to attend to the needs and culture of the participants in preparing the celebration and to give the common spiritual good of the people top priority. The GIRM text is worth quoting in full:

> The pastoral effectiveness of a celebration will be greatly increased if the texts of the readings, the prayers, and the liturgical chants correspond as aptly as possible to the needs, the preparation, and the culture of the participants. This will be achieved by appropriate use of the many possibilities of choice described below.
>
> Hence in arranging the celebration of Mass, the Priest should be *attentive rather to the common spiritual good of the People of God than to his own inclinations*. He should also remember that choices of this kind are to be made in harmony with those who exercise some part in the celebration,

including the faithful, as regards the parts that more directly pertain to them.[14]

We will follow up on some details of these recommendations in a moment. At this point it is important to note the priority that the GIRM places on the common spiritual good of the people and on ministerial collaboration in choosing apt elements of the celebration. The presider, homilist, and all who have a hand in preparing the liturgy have to first listen to what all those who companion their people can tell them about that common spiritual good. It is also important that they have become aware of how catechists have helped people bring their own life stories and spiritual journey into the mystery of dying and rising with Christ into conversation with the day's Scripture readings. In a word, they need to ask the questions of the pastoral companioning and word ministries.

Anticipating Mystagogy and Mission

As we noted earlier, Thomas Morris recommends that those engaged in one form of ministry need to ask not only their own question but also those of the other ministries. In addition to the questions of pastoral companions and ministers of the word, liturgists also need to ask the questions of the mystagogy and mission to follow.

The reason for asking the question for mystagogy can be stated simply. The liturgical event lays a foundation for mystagogical catechesis. It can, in fact, be called a "first mystagogy," for that is where mystagogy begins.[15] The question for liturgists is this: how can we craft a liturgy with

14. General Instruction of the Roman Missal, 352, emphasis added; https://www.usccb.org/prayer-and-worship/the-mass/general -instruction-of-the-roman-missal/girm-chapter-7.

15. See Gilbert Ostdiek, "Liturgy as Catechesis for Life," *The Living Light* 37, no. 4 (Summer 2001): 45–54; "Ongoing Mystagogy Begins in the Liturgy," *Pastoral Music* 25, no. 6 (August–September 2001): 21–22.

Table 61

mystagogical potential? The homily and other moments in the rite where the presider may use "these or similar words" can become such "mystagogical moments." The musical choices to be made throughout the liturgy also have special mystagogical potential.[16] Similarly, because liturgical celebration concludes with a sending, liturgists need to ask themselves the mission question: to what and for what are people being sent back into life beyond the liturgy?

Reweaving Strategies

Ministry at the eucharistic table occupies a privileged place for weaving together both ministries of companioning and word that have gone before and the ministries of mystagogy and mission that follow. By their way of life and their actions pastoral ministers, as well as others of the community of disciples, have helped those they serve to discover Christ's presence in their lives and his call to a new way of living. It is at the eucharistic table that Christ's presence to them takes on a new and powerful form. They now encounter Christ in the bread and wine, the symbols of his total self-giving in love. At this point in the reweaving, the cross-ministry questions of Thomas Morris[17] might well be these: How is Christ present in their daily lives as disciples as they come to the table? What moments of dying and rising do they bring to the Eucharist? How can word and sacrament be opened up to name and deepen that experience? How

16. Regarding the music, which SC 112 calls an "integral part of the liturgy," see Edward Foley, "Musical Mystagogy: A Mystagogy of the Moment," in *Finding Voice to Give God Praise: Essays in the Many Languages of Liturgy*, ed. Kathleen Hughes (Collegeville, MN: Liturgical Press, 1998), 276–87; Edward Foley, "Music and Spirituality—Introduction," *Religions* 6, no. 2 (June 2015): 638–41.

17. Thomas H. Morris, "Liturgical Catechesis Revisited," *Catechumenate* 17, no. 3 (May 1994): 12–19, here at 16.

can they come to know Christ now in the breaking of the bread? How can the Eucharist transform them and set their hearts on fire to be sent on mission? Given the pivotal role the gathering at the eucharistic table plays in the Emmaus story and in our pastoral ministry,[18] rather than focus on detailed pastoral strategies in answer to those questions, we will center our attention here on some of the deeper theological underpinnings on which it is important to base those pastoral practices.

Theologically, the most important parts of eucharistic celebrations are the Liturgy of the Word and the Liturgy of the Eucharist. Pastorally, however, the gathering and sending rites play critically important roles. They are the bridge enabling people to cross from life into liturgy and from liturgy back into life, to bring life into liturgy and the liturgy into life.[19] What can be done pastorally to help them make that connection?[20]

---

18. Celebration of the sacraments, especially the Eucharist, have great formative power (SC 33, 48, 59) and are occasions for widest pastoral care and formation of the greatest number of the faithful. A recent study by Lauren F. Winner, *The Dangers of Christian Practice: On Wayward Gifts, Characteristic Damage, and Sin* (New Haven, CT: Yale University Press, 2018), offers a salutary reminder that liturgical practices can not only form but also deform. Symbols can have a shadow side.

19. On the life-liturgy-life continuity, see Karl Rahner, "How to Receive a Sacrament and Mean It," *Theology Digest* 19 (1971): 227–34, on what he calls "the liturgy of the world," and Ion Bria, "The Liturgy after the Liturgy," *International Review of Mission* 67, no. 265 (January 1978): 86–90.

20. For extensive pastoral reflections on the individual elements of celebration of the Eucharist, see *Introduction to the Order of Mass: A Pastoral Resource of the Bishops' Committee on the Liturgy* (Washington, DC: USCCB, 2003). For fuller mystagogical reflections on individual parts of the Eucharist, see Gilbert Ostdiek, "A Mystagogy of the Eucharist," *Liturgical Ministry* 20, no. 4 (Fall 2011): 161–66; and *Mystagogy of the Eucharist: A Resource for Faith Formation* (Collegeville, MN: Liturgical Press, 2015), the "Background Briefing" sections in chapters 3–9.

Table 63

Let's start first with the processions at the beginning and end of the liturgy, for they are the two-way bridge between life and liturgy. In the entrance procession, a representative few enter the assembly in the name of us all. They carry cross, candles, and Gospel Book. Each of these tell the story not only of Christ but also of the entire assembly. The one who journeyed to Calvary said: "Take up the cross and follow me" (Matt 16:24; Mark 8:34; Luke 9:23; 14:27). The one who is the light of the world said: "You are the light of the world"; do not hide it; rather, let it give light to all (Matt 5:14-16; Luke 11:33-35). And the Gospel Book tells us that the one who served and showed the greatest love said: "For I have set you an example, that you also should do as I have done to you" (John 13:15) and "I give you a new commandment, that you love one another. Just as I have loved you, you also should love one another" (John 13:34). Those three symbols brought into the assembly in solemn procession tell Christ's disciples what the Eucharist is about, what all their lives are about. All of us should be walking in that procession, at least in spirit, bringing in our work and our lives.

The sending is less elaborate but no less significant. Transformed by the celebration of word and table, we are blessed and sent back into our lives of discipleship in the world, to take up our daily dying and rising with Christ, to be light to others, to serve in love, to be his "silent witnesses" in the world.[21] The gathering area (narthex) then becomes the sending area. Only a representative few leave the assembly in that final procession, but we should all know that we are

---

21. The church documents on evangelization all speak of "silent proclamation" by all the baptized as the first and absolutely nonnegotiable requirement for the subsequent official activities of the church: i.e., missionary activity (explicit proclamation), initiatory activity (forming Christian communities), and pastoral activity (pastoral care of those communities).

marching out with them to take up our work and our lives of service in the world.

These two processions deserve the best pastoral care we can give them, in ritual performance and in choice of songs that accompany these actions. Both processions serve to link liturgy and life, to weave together the ministries that precede and follow them. If we are to reweave table ministry with those ministries, collaboration and listening to their questions are imperative.

In the Liturgy of the Word, we note only two things.[22] First, the enthronement of the Gospel Book on the altar until it is taken up for proclamation makes a visual connection between ambo and table, a twofold manifestation of Christ's active presence in the assembly.[23] The rituals surrounding the proclamation of the gospel stress the presence and action of Christ. The ritual dialogue and signing oneself at the gospel both affirm that Christ leads and accompanies us on our life journey to the cross. For that reason these ritual actions deserve careful pastoral attention, performance, and choice of sung acclamation suited to the context and spiritual needs of the assembly.

The procession with the gifts is also of great "spiritual significance,"[24] for as the prayers of blessing over them proclaim, the bread and wine are not only gifts of God and earth, field and vine; they are also condensed symbols, the

22. As also their harmonious design (*General Introduction to the Lectionary for Mass* 32).

23. SC 56 notes that "the liturgy of the word and the liturgy of the eucharist are so closely connected with each other that they form but one single act of worship." It is Christ who speaks when the gospel is proclaimed (SC 7), and the Rite of Dedication of an Altar notes that "Christian writers see in the altar a sign of Christ himself—hence they affirm: 'The altar is Christ'" (Dedication of an Altar 4, in *Dedication of a Church and an Altar*).

24. See GIRM 73.

Table 65

gift of all the human work that produces them. They are gifts of our work, our lives, our world. Along with those representative few who present them, we should all walk in spirit, carrying in our hands the gift of our lives and work, to lay them on the altar for transformation. How can the demeanor of the gift-bearers and the song we sing to accompany them convey the spiritual meaning of what we are all doing? That too deserves our pastoral care.

The Eucharistic Prayer is "the center and high point of the entire celebration" (GIRM 78). We have already reflected on the words of Jesus over the bread and wine and his command. Here I will highlight only two themes voiced immediately after the institution account. First, in the memorial and offering (technically called anamnesis and oblation), Eucharistic Prayer III proclaims, "we offer you in thanksgiving this holy and living sacrifice." "Living sacrifice" is New Testament code language for Christian life (e.g., Rom 12:1). We now offer what we had earlier placed on the altar, the gift of daily life and "our very selves" (SC 48; GIRM 79e-f), now offered along with Jesus' offering of himself.[25] If only we could affirm this pivotal moment immediately with an acclamation. Second, we immediately ask God to accept our offering and transform us, so that, "filled with his Holy Spirit, [we] may become one body, one spirit in Christ" (EP III). Our very lives are transformed with Christ into living worship, into a gift of self out of love. This

---

25. There is a marvelous parallel here. Edward Schillebeeckx writes that the death of Jesus, which we consider the supreme act of worship, was not a cultic act celebrated in a temple by an authorized Jewish Levite or priest but rather a public execution. It is, in fact, "secular worship"; his offering of his life is itself an act of worship. See Schillebeeckx, "Secular Worship and Church Liturgy," in his *God the Future of Man*, trans. N. D. Smith (New York: Sheed and Ward, 1968), 91–116. So too is our self-offering secular worship, our living sacrifice (see LG 34).

moment of making a twofold offering is affirmed by the triple Amen at the end of the Eucharistic Prayer.

The Rite of Communion has many rich themes. Here we will focus on two. After the exchange of peace and breaking of the bread, we form a procession to the table. Unlike the other processions, all are invited to come to the table, to receive into our hands the Holy Gifts for the Holy People. The ritual dialogue—"The Body of Christ" "Amen"—has a twofold meaning in 1 Corinthians: the eucharistic Body of Christ (11:24) and the Body of Christ that is the church (10:16-17). Commenting on this epistle, St. Augustine put it simply: "Receive what you are, become what you receive."[26] We say "Amen" to both receiving and being the Body of Christ.[27] We are then sent to be that Body of Christ to the world.

The celebration of the Eucharist condenses into itself the entire Emmaus narrative. The heart of the liturgy is the celebration of the mystery of Christ, summed up especially in the paschal mystery of his passion, death, and resurrection (SC 2, 5, 61). The Eucharist rehearses the life-death-life pattern of Jesus and invites disciples, again and again, to journey into the paschal mystery pattern of life-death-newness-of-life in communion with him. Strategies for weaving eucharistic table ministry into the other ministries should be rooted in that theological vision. They should be planned and performed as authentically, fully, and prayerfully as possible.

---

26. A common paraphrasing based on a fuller statement in Sermon 272 of St. Augustine.

27. The invitation "The Body of Christ" honors that twofold meaning. The current practice of approaching the table in a single-file procession, however, does not capture this dual meaning as fully as would approaching to receive together in small groups of two or more.

Table 67

Summary Reflection

Guiding others into a relationship of communion with Christ is woven into all the ministries. Ministers of pastoral companioning and word have helped them discover Christ's presence and call in their lives. It is at the eucharistic table that Christ's presence to them takes on a new and powerful form. It is there that they can again come to know Christ in the breaking of the bread and have their hearts set on fire for the mission on which they are sent.

5
Mystagogy

Emmaus Story

[32]They said to each other, "Were not our hearts burning within us while he was talking to us on the road, while he was opening up the scriptures to us?"

Paradigm for Ministry

In keeping with the flow of the Emmaus account, we now turn our attention to the next moment on the journey of the two disciples. They had gone through a kaleidoscope of experiences: a bitter tale of lost faith and hope; the stranger's heartwarming retelling of that story now ending in glory, attested by Moses and all the prophets; and then a meal prayer revealing the stranger to them as the Lord, alive and table host for them. Only now can they look back and put into words, in one brief yet powerful sentence, how the stranger's story had set their "hearts burning" on the way (Luke 24:32).[1] That verse is a perfect description of what mystagogy does. It helps people to name their experience and see more deeply into what it means.[2]

1. In a lovely turn of phrase, theologian-poet John Shea names the stranger the "arsonist of the heart," in his *The Hour of the Unexpected* (Niles, IL: Argus Communications, 1977), 49.
2. For fuller details on mystagogy and its place within liturgical cate-chesis, see the technical note in appendix 2 at the end of this book.

Throughout his public ministry, Jesus was adept at drawing listeners deeper into the meaning of their lives and their Scriptures. The language and experience of "opening up" Scriptures, hearts, and eyes (vv. 31, 32, 45) offers us a starting point for this phase of our paradigm. A few examples of how Jesus leads his hearers from experience, real or imagined, or from Scriptures to a message that had lain hidden for them will suffice.

The use of parables is one of Jesus' favorite ways of teaching. To his disciples, Jesus explains the purpose of using parables: "To you it has been given to know the secrets of the kingdom of God; but to others I speak in parables, so that 'looking they may not perceive and listening they may not understand'" (Luke 8:10; also Matt 13:13; Mark 4:12). For that reason, he tells parables to all who gather to hear him and later explains them to the disciples privately: for example, the sower and the seed (Luke 8:4-8 and 11-15; Matt 13:1-9 and 18-23; Mark 4:1-9 and 13-20), the wheat and the weeds (Matt 13:24-30 and 36-43), the mustard seed (Mark 4:30-32 and 33-34), and the dishonest steward (Luke 16:1-8 and 9-13).

In other instances, Jesus cites a Scripture passage and interprets its meaning with a gloss: for example, the reading from Isaiah 61:1-2 and his commentary on it in his hometown synagogue (Luke 4:16-21). Think of the series of his reinterpretations of received traditions in the Sermon on the Mount: "you have heard it said . . . but I say to you . . ." (Matt 5:21-48). Or his extended midrashic interpretation of the manna in his Bread of Life discourse (John 6:30-59). Or, to return to our story, how he opens up to the disciples on the way to Emmaus the message about himself in "Moses and all the prophets" (Luke 24:25, 27).[3]

---

3. That opening up of the Scriptures on the way might be seen as a mystagogical prelude to the later naming of the fire in their hearts.

It would be anachronistic to say that this method used by Jesus should be called mystagogy. Yet there is a thread that runs through his way of teaching that was quickly followed in the early church, a movement from a first hearing of the kerygma to a deeper and more reflective spiritual understanding. For example, consider Peter's Pentecost proclamation of the kerygma and subsequent elaboration of it (Acts 2:14-36 and 38-40) and the episode of Philip and the Ethiopian (Acts 8:26-36). That methodological thread[4] also anticipates what was later developed and woven into the catechumenal process in the third to fifth centuries when it became known as mystagogy.[5]

However we name it, by his words and actions the stranger has given his two companions on the way the mystagogue's gift of being enabled to name the fire burning in their hearts and to act on it.

Connecting the Ministries

How, then, can we draw out the flow of mystagogy from word and table and then forward to the ministry of mission that will follow?

Building on Word and Table

Naming the fire in their hearts would not have been possible for the two disciples if they had not recognized him in the breaking of the bread, and their hearts would not have been

---

4. The movement from first kerygma to a deeper understanding might well fit Paul's analogy of feeding the Corinthians first with milk and then with solid food (1 Cor 3:2).

5. The intent here is not to argue for a genetic development to patristic mystagogy. For a fuller treatment of mystagogy, see the note in appendix 2 at the end of this book. Also see Gil Ostdiek, *Mystagogy of the Eucharist: A Resource for Faith Formation* (Collegeville, MN: Liturgical Press, 2015), 6–10.

set on fire if he had not joined them on the way, listened to their story, and given them a new ending for it. Mystagogy, then, builds on what has gone before, on word and table.

In the previous chapter we noted that mystagogy actually begins in the Eucharist. The Eucharist is itself a first mystagogy. That is accomplished in several key ways. First, and most obvious, one such key is a homily carefully prepared in a dialogue between the story told in the readings and the stories of hearers' concerns and experiences.[6] The homily breaks open the meaning the biblical story has for our lives, or rather, it opens up the biblical story so we can hear our life stories in it. It helps us hear Christ present and speaking to us in the Gospel (SC 7).

Music provides another mystagogical key in the liturgy.[7] Music brings its own unique mystagogical potential to the ritual actions it accompanies. The meaning of the sound is found in the performance and lies beyond what words can express; the words of songs are best when poetic and metaphoric in nature, beyond exact analysis. Music's meaning is elusive; it is both heard and hidden. Live music is sound in motion; it is performed, not static. It condenses the journeying of life into the duration of the song. It is a mystagogy of the moment, preserved only in memory. Given these characteristics, it is no wonder that music is such an "effective means for communicating with a God who is both present and hidden . . . a powerful symbol for the Divine

---

6. That happens readily in the homily preparation groups recommended by *Fulfilled in Your Hearing: The Homily in the Sunday Assembly* (Washington, DC: USCCB, 1982), 36, https://www.usccb.org/beliefs-and-teachings/vocations/priesthood/priestly-life-and-ministry/upload/fiyh.pdf.

7. See Edward Foley, "Musical Mystagogy: A Mystagogy of the Moment," in *Finding Voice to Give God Praise: Essays in the Many Languages of Liturgy*, ed. Kathleen Hughes (Collegeville, MN: Liturgical Press, 1998), 276–87.

Self who is recognizable while remaining the unnamable 'I am who I am' (Exod 3:14)."[8] The mystagogical potential of liturgical music is probably one of the richest resources of liturgical mystagogy in a celebration because of the wide array of hymns and songs available for selection. Both lyrics and musical style can open ritual actions in the liturgy to deeper attention and reflection and make them memorable. And even though the words to be sung in the Order of Mass are fixed, the choice of musical style and setting still allow for mystagogy to be at work there as well.

Another, more subtle key is found in the ritual symbols. We believe that "by his power Christ is present in the sacraments" and acting "by means of signs perceptible to the senses, which signify and bring about human sanctification in ways proper to each of these signs; in the liturgy the whole public worship is performed by the Mystical Body of Jesus Christ, that is, by the Head and his members" (SC 7). This foundational understanding of the ritual symbols of liturgy received a much fuller explanation in the *Catechism of the Catholic Church*, which was approved by John Paul II in 1992 and published in English translation in 1994.[9] The *Catechism's* elaboration of this conciliar foundation offers liturgists and catechists an important way of thinking about the ritual symbols for the practice of both celebration and mystagogy of the liturgy. For that reason we will take a closer look at what the *Catechism* says about ritual symbols.

The opening statement of the theme is compelling: "A sacramental celebration is woven from signs and symbols. . . . [T]heir meaning is rooted in the work of creation

---

8. See Edward Foley, "Music as Sound Spirituality," *The Way Supplement* 96 (Fall 1999): 56–64, here at 59.

9. John Paul II, *Catechism of the Catholic Church* (New York: William H. Sadlier Inc., 1994).

and in human culture, specified by events of the Old Covenant and fully revealed in the person and work of Christ" (CCC 1145). That meaning is first established and then transformed through several levels of symbolism, built up in:

– Signs of the human world (1146–49);

– Signs of the covenant (1150);

– Signs taken up by Christ (1151); and

– Sacramental signs (1152).

CCC then concludes in brief:

The liturgical celebration involves signs and symbols relating to

– creation (candles, water, fire),

– human life (washing, anointing, breaking bread),

– the history of salvation (rites of Passover).

– Integrated into the world of faith and taken up by the power of the Holy Spirit, these cosmic elements, human rituals, and gestures of remembrance of God become bearers of the saving and sanctifying action of Christ. (1189)[10]

The last line could be rephrased as

– the fulfillment of salvation history in Christ (sacramental rites of remembrance).

Why is the CCC schema important for liturgy and mystagogy? Both stand to gain immensely from careful attention

___

10. This indented paragraph is a direct quotation, formatted in sense lines to emphasize the layering of symbols.

to these layers that make up the ritual symbols. Starting from the cosmic level of creation and moving up through the subsequent layers of human ritual, Jewish rites of remembrance, and Christian sacramental rites of remembrance, the symbol's meaning is "being put/thrown together" (the literal meaning of symbol, *sym-ballein*); its meaning on the base level is both retained and yet transformed more deeply at every level until our ritual symbols "become bearers of the saving and sanctifying action of Christ." The formative power of liturgy depends on how well we perform the liturgy at every one of those levels: robust and abundant cosmic elements (water, oil, bread and wine), fulsome and familiar human ritual actions (washing, anointing, eating and drinking) carefully and prayerfully performed with a sense of Christ's presence (not in a slovenly or careless manner), and the Christ story told powerfully in word proclaimed and broken open in the words and ritual actions of remembrance.

This is an initial mystagogy that speaks for itself or, rather, sets hearts on fire. The ritual symbols themselves become silent mystagogues. And that gives the structured mystagogy to follow a head start for naming the experience and relating the sacramental symbols to their roots in nature, human life, the life of our ancestors in faith, and the life and actions of Christ. And wonder of wonders, it is through such ordinary and daily things that we come to know that God is present and at work in our lives.

At the same time, the "silent mystagogy" of the ritual symbols works in the other direction as well. As the actions and things of ordinary human life are drawn into God's action in the liturgy, they are also opened up as the place of God's presence in our everyday lives and world. This can overturn many supposed dichotomies between "sacred" and "profane." They tell us that ordinary ways of relating with family and friends—at meals and in so many other

ways—can be holy too, and they provision the work of sacramental catechesis with a wealth of ways to open up the
meaning of the sacraments.

In sum, a liturgical celebration that is both fully human
and palpably holy in its prayerful performance is already
a first mystagogy. In connecting liturgy to ordinary life in
the world, such mystagogy also opens up a way for us to
be sent back into that world with a mission to discover the
holiness and presence of God in our lives.

Leading to Mission

Celebrations of the Eucharist, and other liturgical celebrations as well, conclude with a blessing and dismissal. We
are sent "so that each may go back to doing good works,
praising and blessing God" (GIRM 90c). This makes explicit
for us the dynamic implied in the Emmaus narrative. The
mystagogical moment of naming the fire in the hearts of the
two disciples (Luke 24:32) links table to mission (v. 33). In
recognizing the risen Lord in the breaking of the bread at
table, they recognize not only that he is alive and here with
them but also that they are still his disciples and that they
are still charged with the mission he had given them. There
could be no hesitation; they had to go back that same night
to tell the others what they had experienced (v. 35). The
explicit dismissal in our celebrations is more than a mere
invitation to disperse, to just go away. It is a sending forth
on mission. More on this in the next chapter.

Reweaving Strategies

Three sets of questions are important for reweaving the
ministry of mystagogy with the surrounding ministries.
What questions should a mystagogue ask of the practitioners of those ministries? To answer these questions dialogue
and collaboration between several areas of pastoral ministry
are critical.

The first question is the liturgical question. Was the liturgy shaped and celebrated with its mystagogical potential in mind? How was that shown specifically? Was the liturgy celebrated in such a way that participants could recognize the presence and action of Christ in their midst and come to know him in the word proclaimed and in the breaking of the bread? Were they sent on mission with hearts set on fire by that moment of rediscovering Christ's abiding promise to be with them always?

Asking the liturgical question falls not only to mystagogues who do follow-up programs of faith formation. It should also be on the minds of those who do preparatory liturgical catechesis. They might take inspiration from the questions posed by Thomas Morris,[11] cited in chapter 1. What can we do to prepare people to celebrate the liturgy with authenticity and integrity? How can we help them to understand the link between life and liturgy? To understand that the little ways of dying to self and rising to new ways of living, day by day, are the gift of self we bring to the table, Sunday by Sunday, to place on the altar and join with the self-offering of Christ? To understand that this way of living is the life task of gospel witness to which the baptized are always sent forth from the liturgy?

The second question to ask, the mystagogical question, should also be a preoccupation of those who prepare and lead the liturgy itself. They are doing first mystagogy. As noted above, homily, ritual symbols, and liturgical music each have significant mystagogical potential and deserve special attention and care.[12] Do each of these in their own

---

11. Thomas H. Morris, "Liturgical Catechesis Revisited," *Catechumenate* 17, no. 3 (May 1994): 12–19, here at 16.

12. Bishops' Committee on the Liturgy, *Environment and Art in Catholic Worship* (Washington, DC: NCCB, 1978), nos. 14–15, in a lovely phrase notes that "renewal requires the opening up of our symbols . . . until we can experience all of them as authentic and appreciate their symbolic value."

way facilitate the meeting between Christ and assembly?
Are our human lives brought into effective communion with
the life of the one whose disciples we are, so that Christ is
known as present to us not only during the time of the liturgy but also as our companion on the way throughout our
daily lives and work? In a word, can the liturgy help us say
with St. Paul, "I have been crucified with Christ; and it is
no longer I who live, but it is Christ who lives in me" (Gal
2:19-20)? Can it help us to take Paul seriously when he says:
"now in the Lord you are light. Live as children of the light"
(Eph 5:8)? Or to accept what Paul envisions: "You your-
selves are our letter . . . to be known and read by all; and
you show that you are a letter of Christ . . . written not with
ink but with the Spirit of the living God, not on tablets of
stone but on tablets of human hearts" (2 Cor 3:2-3)?[13] Do
we not affirm all that when we carry cross, candles, and
Gospel Book into the assembly as we gather and then back
out into the world as we are sent?

The third question is the mission question. Mystagogues,
whether the liturgists who shape and lead the celebration
of the liturgy or those who engage in subsequent catechesis
for continuing faith formation, also need to query those who
minister in various forms of gospel mission to which we
are each sent. How can liturgical celebration and subsequent
faith formation help enkindle and fan in our hearts the fire
that will impel all of us to become what Pope Francis has
described as "missionary disciples"?[14] How can liturgical

13. Leslie Newbigin once wrote: "Christians are a hermeneutic of the
Gospel, and for many people it's the only Gospel they will ever read."
See *The Gospel in a Pluralistic Society* (Grand Rapids, MI: William B.
Eerdmans, 1989), 227. Roman documents on mission call this "silent
proclamation."

14. Pope Francis, Apostolic Exhortation *Evangelii Gaudium* (2013), 120.
We noted earlier that Anthony Gittins simply names disciples are those
who are "called to be sent." In *Called to Be Sent: Co-Missioned as Disciples*

celebration and ongoing mystagogy help spread that missionary fire into concrete ways of acting, whether small or large, to transform our worlds and to bring gospel values to address the issues we face today?

Finally, despite its brevity, the rite of dismissal does offer in liturgical practice several possibilities for mystagogy. One such moment is the wording of the dismissal itself. Commenting on *Ite missa est*, Benedict XVI reminds us that "[t]hese few words succinctly express the missionary nature of the Church. The People of God might be helped to understand more clearly this essential dimension of the Church's life, taking the dismissal as a starting-point."[15] There is food here for a follow-up mystagogical catechesis that opens up the progression from Mass to mission. A pastoral letter of Cardinal Joseph Bernardin gives us a superb example of this when he writes: "The dismissal of the assembly is like the breaking of the bread. We have become 'the bread of life' and the 'cup of blessing' for the world. Now we are scattered, broken, poured out to be life for the world. What happens at home, at work, at meals? What do we make of our time, our words, our deeds, our resources of all kinds? That is what matters."[16]

Follow-up mystagogical catechesis on the final blessing could reflect profitably on the final ritual action of the blessing and signing of oneself. Commenting on this action, Susan Roll writes: "The cross represents our identity as the baptized people of God who have died and risen with Christ and are now, personally and communally, configured to Christ. While at the beginning [of the liturgy] this expression

---

Today (Liguori, MO: Liguori Publications, 2008), 4, he writes: "we are '*co-missioned*' by the one who is the true subject of mission."

15. Benedict XVI, Postsynodal Apostolic Exhortation *Sacramentum Caritatis* (2007), 51.

16. Cardinal Joseph Bernardin, *Guide for the Assembly* (Chicago: Liturgy Training Publications, 1997), no. 79.

of our identity marked the depth of our common call to be *ekklesia*, at the conclusion of the liturgy we carry this identity, as problematic as it might become in the concrete and challenging circumstances of our lives, into the larger domain in which we live."[17]

Another mystagogical moment is the choice of a song often sung after the concluding rite.[18] Lyrics of the song, or a marching melody, can be chosen to send the worshipers back into mission in their lives. It also helps to think of the narthex not only as the place of gathering but also as the place of sending. One church has placed the words "servant entrance" inside and above the main doors for all to see as they go forth.[19]

Summary Reflection

Communion with Christ is the basic priority woven into all the ministries. Mystagogy forms a bridge from the previous ministries and fires the imagination for disciples to go forth on mission into the world as the Body of Christ, to invite others into that communion.

17. Susan K. Roll, "Theology and the Latin Text and Rite," in *A Commentary on the Order of Mass of the Roman Missal*, ed. Edward Foley (Collegeville, MN: Liturgical Press, 2011), 635–37, here at 636.

18. *Music in Catholic Worship* notes that "a recessional song is optional" (49), though it is not mentioned in the GIRM.

19. I have often wondered whether the mystagogical potential of the narthex as the place of being sent forth might also be expressed ritually by enshrining the processional cross, candles, and Gospel Book there for us to reverence as we depart and to remind us of the way of life to which we are again being sent on mission. This would blend well with the mystagogical comment of Roll, above.

6
Mission

Emmaus Story

[33]That same hour they got up and returned to Jerusalem; and they found the eleven and their companions gathered together. [34]They were saying, "The Lord has risen indeed, and he has appeared to Simon!" [35]Then they told what had happened on the road, and how he had been made known to them in the breaking of the bread.

Paradigm for Ministry

The final scene of the Emmaus account finds the two disciples immediately retracing their steps and returning to Jerusalem, bubbling over with good news to tell the other disciples gathered there (Luke 24:33). That the others already knew the good news (v. 34) could not stifle the two returnees from Emmaus. They had a mission to carry out;[1] the story of their experience could not be left untold. So they

---

1. Luke's narrative does not include an explicit act of sending the two disciples on mission by the risen Lord. As noted in chapters 4 and 5, however, it would follow implicitly. His heartwarming retelling of their experience and letting himself be known in the breaking of the bread revived their call to discipleship. It seems logical to see in that restoration of their discipleship an implicit renewal of the mission he had given them earlier. Other resurrection appearances to the women who visited the

recounted what had happened on the road and how the stranger was made known to them as the risen Lord when he broke the bread for them (v. 35). With this simple narrative stroke, "Luke transforms a traditional recognition story of the risen Lord into a blueprint for christian mission."[2]

In the first scene of the Emmaus account the two disciples had succinctly summarized the first portion of the early kerygma, the blueprint that underlies the gospel accounts of the earthly ministry of Jesus. Those accounts unfold fully the blueprint that is the model for the rewoven pastoral ministry we have been tracing in the previous chapters. One unifying thread woven through the full gospel accounts of Jesus' mission can be captured in the verb "send" (*mittere / missio* in Latin, *apostellō* in Greek[3]). Notice how often and in how many contexts this verb is used in the New Testament. Note too how sending marks successive phases in the unfolding pattern of Jesus' mission.

Again and again Jesus identifies himself not as the originator of his mission but as one "sent" by God, "the one who sent me" (e.g., Matt 10:40; Mark 9:37; Luke 10:16; John 5:36, 38; 6:57; 7:29; 8:42; 11:42; 17:3, 21). Jesus was sent so "that the world might be saved through him" (John 3:17). When Jesus publicly took up that saving mission before his hometown people, he presented himself as fulfilling the words of Isaiah about being anointed and sent to carry out God's saving plan (Luke 4:18-21).

---

tomb include an explicit mission to "go quickly and tell his disciples" (Matt 28:7; Mark 16:7).

2. James B. Dunning, *Echoing God's Word: Formation for Catechists and Homilists in a Catechumenal Church* (Arlington, VA: The North American Forum on the Catechumenate, 1993), 291.

3. Also transliterated into English as "apostle." In Luke's gospel "apostle" and "the twelve" are at times used synonymously, in contrast to a more inclusive usage of "sending" in the other gospels.

Clearly, then, Jesus sees that his mission begins from God.[4] Mission is God's initiative, and its full realization by Jesus is actually God's doing. "He whom God has sent speaks the words of God" (John 3:34); "My teaching is not my own, but his who sent me" (7:16; also 8:26; 12:49). In John's Gospel, Jesus is the Word of God who speaks the words of God. The same can also be said of all that Jesus does in carrying out his mission. "Very truly, I tell you, the Son can do nothing on his own, but only what he sees the Father doing; for whatever the Father does, the Son does likewise" (John 5:19). His mission is God's mission. "The works that the Father has given me to complete, the very works that I am doing, testify on my behalf that the Father has sent me" (John 5:36; also 17:4). Jesus' mission is to carry out God's mission, the *missio Dei*.[5]

In carrying out this mission, Jesus announces, by word and by works of healing, mercy, forgiveness, and inclusion, the breaking in of God's reign. But that is not to be Jesus' work alone. He entrusts it to his followers. The way of life in that reign he teaches and models is not just for the sole benefit of individuals; they are enjoined to "let your light shine before others, so that they may see your good works and give glory to your Father in heaven" (Matt 5:16). Their lives are to be a witness given through their good works, what church documents now call "silent proclamation."[6]

---

4. See *Ad Gentes* 2: God's saving plan "flows from the 'fount-like love' or charity of God the Father" out into "the mission of the Son and the mission of the Holy Spirit." It is from that twofold mission of God that the church draws its origin, making the church "missionary by nature." Contemporary theology of mission roots mission in God's mission (*missio Dei*).

5. As noted in chapter 1, the mission of God is the bedrock of the ministry of Jesus, and total commitment to that mission is characteristic of the entire ministry of Jesus. More on the *missio Dei* in appendix 3 at the end of the book.

6. As noted earlier, Roman documents see this "silent proclamation" as the first and absolutely indispensable step for all evangelization and

Jesus' sense of the urgency of his mission often surfaces in a favorite image of his. "The harvest is plentiful, but the laborers are few" (Matt 9:37; Luke 10:2). It is a harvest that must be gathered in immediately, lest it be lost. The good news must be spread, not only by the silent proclamation of living witness, but also by explicit proclamation. Accordingly, Jesus invites others to join in his mission work. He first gathers followers to go with him to hear his teaching and witness his works. In a kind of apprenticeship, he models for them his message and the way they are to follow.[7] From among them he chooses twelve and sends them to help him carry on his mission, to be his coworkers (Matt 10:5; Mark 3:14; Luke 9:2). They are sent to "proclaim the good news . . . cure the sick, raise the dead, cleanse the lepers, cast out demons" (Matt 10:7-8). He sends them out to say and do all that he says and does, just as he says and does all that his Abba has given him to say and do.

When Jesus leaves his home region of Galilee on his teaching journey to Jerusalem, Luke recounts that he first sends messengers and then an additional seventy disciples "ahead of him in pairs to every town and place where he himself intended to go" because "the harvest is plentiful, but the laborers are few" (Luke 10:1-2). It is so urgent that if they are not received in a town, they are to wipe the dust of that place off their feet and go on to the next one (10:10-11). Those sent are to go in pairs.[8] Mission is not an individual enterprise;

---

subsequent ecclesial activity in forming and caring for Christian communities (EN 21; also AG 11–12; MR 42–43).

7. Jesus is the way (John 14:6), and his followers were first known as those who "belonged to the way" before they were called Christians (Acts 9:2 and 11:26).

8. Luke does not say how the pairs were chosen. Self-selected by kinship or friendship? Paired by Jesus as he sent them because of the complementarity of their individual gifts for the task of mission? The latter method would make sense in our context.

it is a collective, collaborative endeavor. Elsewhere Jesus reminds the Twelve that coworkers may not always live to see the fruits of their work. "For here the saying holds true, 'One sows and another reaps.' I sent you to reap that for which you did not labor. Others have labored, and you have entered into their labor" (John 4:37-38). Mission, then, is a collaborative effort that stretches over time. It is done together and handed on to others as time goes by.

Being sent on mission is the legacy Jesus leaves to his disciples. At the Last Supper, as he faces his imminent death, Jesus offers a final prayer for the disciples to his Father: "As you have sent me into the world, so I have sent them into the world" (John 17:18). That sending continues immediately after his death. When Mary Magdalene and the other Mary visit the tomb, an angel tells them to "go quickly and tell his disciples, 'He has been raised from the dead, and indeed he is going ahead of you to Galilee; there you will see him.' This is my message for you" (Matt 28:7-8). John's Gospel has a slightly different take. When Mary Magdalene visits the empty tomb, she encounters someone she first believes to be the gardener. When he reveals himself as the risen Lord, he himself delivers the message and instructs her to "go to my brothers and say to them, 'I am ascending to my Father and your Father, to my God and your God'" (John 20:17). Mary Magdalene went and told the disciples, becoming known thereafter as the "apostle to the apostles."

Later that same day, the risen Lord appears to the disciples themselves, huddling in fear behind locked doors, and once more he personally hands over to them the mission he had received: "As the Father has sent me, so I send you" (John 20:21). God's mission is to continue. It is to be handed on to others in turn: "Go therefore and make disciples of all nations" (Matt 28:19). In the final chapters of Luke's Gospel, that mission ripples out in concentric circles. The women go to the tomb and return to the other disciples.

Two disciples then journey farther, to Emmaus and back to Jerusalem. Now in his final appearance to them before his ascension, the risen Lord sends the disciples forth from Jerusalem to their mission without any boundary restrictions at all.[9] The good news of "repentance and forgiveness of sins is to be proclaimed in his name to all nations, beginning from Jerusalem" (Luke 24:47). In Matthew's Gospel the heart of that mission sending is summed up by one main verb: "make disciples of all nations" (Matt 28:19). Disciple making is the co-mission on which they are sent.[10]

The Emmaus narrative is thus a condensed summary of the blueprint for all Christian mission. Sending is a thread that runs throughout and binds it together, from God's sending of Jesus, to his sending of the disciples during his earthly ministry, to his final post-resurrection sending of disciples to all the nations. That handing on of mission still goes on for us today. We are all co-missioned, together with one another and with him. The final overarching goal of all pastoral ministry is to "make disciples" and form them to spread to all the world the *missio Dei* brought to fulfillment by the one God sent. This offers us valuable principles for our reweaving of the ministries:

- *Missio Dei*, at the heart of all mission, is the work of God, who invites all into a communion of love shown to others in self-giving service, mercy, and forgiveness.

- The mission of Jesus is to bring that love down to earth.

- Every disciple is called to be sent on mission, co-missioned to act in his name, not their own.

9. This is to continue the boundary-crossing characteristic of the ministry of Jesus himself, noted in chapter 1.

10. Translated literally, the great commission reads: "Going therefore, make disciples [*mathēteusate*] of all nations, baptizing them . . . and teaching them to obey everything that I have commanded you" (Matt 28:19-20)—one main verb with three accompanying participles.

- The goal of all official pastoral ministry is to form disciples for that mission.[11]

- Because ministers act in the name of Jesus[12] and because they all minister to the integral journey of disciples on the way, they are to work collaboratively.

- Ministers carry out their particular role in God's mission with coworkers for a time and pass it on to their successors like a baton.

- Pastoral ministry moves from companioning to sending and then back to companioning in a continuing spiral.

Connecting the Ministries

To draw out the connections, we need to reflect briefly on two questions. How does mystagogy flow into mission? And to what does mission then lead?

From Mystagogy to Mission

First a word about mission. When we hear the words "mission" or "missionaries" we usually think of those who are sent to work among faraway peoples who have not yet heard the Gospel or been baptized or to care for them once they have become Christians. We think of those who do this work (missionaries), what they do (evangelize), and where they do it (in "the missions"). For our purposes, mission is being taken in a broader sense. Mission is the calling all

---

11. For further reflection on the relation between mission and ministry, see appendix 3 at the end of this book.

12. We are accustomed to think of priests as those who act in the name of Jesus, *in persona Christi*. Regarding catechesis, the *Catechism of the Catholic Church* 427 writes: "In catechesis . . . it is Christ alone who teaches—anyone else teaches to the extent that he [*sic*] is Christ's spokesman [*sic*], enabling Christ to teach with his [*sic*] lips."

disciples receive in baptism, renewed at the end of every celebration of the Eucharist, to work for the coming of God's reign. Mission is part and parcel of what it means to be church, as Benedict XVI has said: "*Ite, missa est.* These words help us to grasp the relationship between the Mass just celebrated and the mission of Christians in the world. In antiquity, *missa* simply meant 'dismissal.' However in Christian usage it gradually took on a deeper meaning. The word 'dismissal' has come to imply a 'mission.' These few words succinctly express the missionary nature of the Church. The People of God might be helped to understand more clearly this essential dimension of the Church's life, taking the dismissal as a starting-point."[13]

How that common mission is carried out is further shaped by the particular state of life to which everyone is called and by the particular gifts the Spirit gives them to address the local needs and issues in their time and place. In his extended treatment of those spiritual gifts (1 Cor 12:1–14:40), Paul insists that all the Spirit's gifts are given not for personal benefit, but for the common good (12:7) and that the greatest gift is love (13:13). The life task of all disciples is to live out in their particular state of life the message of God's love made known and offered to all by Christ at the great price of his death. The first letter of John puts it simply: "since God loved us so much, we also ought to love one another" (1 John 4:11). Spreading that love is at the heart of Christ's mission, the *missio Dei.*

As noted above, that mission begins with the common task of being living witnesses. In *Evangelii Nuntiandi* 21, Paul VI puts that in plain but compelling words worth quoting in full:

---

13. Benedict XVI, Postsynodal Apostolic Exhortation *Sacramentum Caritatis* 51, http://www.vatican.va/content/benedict-xvi/en/apost _exhortations/documents/hf_ben-xvi_exh_20070222_sacramentum -caritatis.html.

Above all the Gospel must be proclaimed by witness. Take a Christian or a handful of Christians who, in the midst of their own community, show their capacity for understanding and acceptance, their sharing of life and destiny with other people, their solidarity with the efforts of all for whatever is noble and good. Let us suppose that, in addition, they radiate in an altogether simple and unaffected way their faith in values that go beyond current values, and their hope in something that is not seen and that one would not dare to imagine. Through this wordless witness these Christians stir up irresistible questions in the hearts of those who see how they live: Why are they like this? Why do they live in this way? What or who is it that inspires them? Why are they in our midst? Such a witness is already a silent proclamation of the Good News and a very powerful and effective one. Here we have an initial act of evangelization.[14]

These plain-sounding words, however, presuppose that such witnesses have been set on fire and energized by an experience compelling enough for them to see and embrace that life task. Was that not the mystagogical "aha" moment the two disciples experienced with the stranger who sat at the Emmaus table with them? Was that not an overwhelming experience of encountering God's self-giving love revealed in Jesus? To again quote Pope Francis: "Every Christian is a missionary to the extent that he or she has encountered the love of God in Christ Jesus: we no longer say that we are 'disciples' and 'missionaries,' but rather that we are always 'missionary disciples.'"[15]

Reweaving mystagogy into mission, then, depends on all that has gone before in an integrated pastoral ministry:

14. These words echo some of the ideas found earlier in AG 11–12.

15. Pope Francis, Apostolic Exhortation *Evangelii Gaudium* 120, http://www.vatican.va/content/francesco/en/apost_exhortations/documents/papa-francesco_esortazione-ap_20131124_evangelii-gaudium.html.

listening to people's stories of deep longing for the presence of God in their lives, helping them find words to understand how that story of longing can find fulfillment and nourishment by the one who speaks those words of love and offers them food for the journey. The moment of mystagogical awakening is the bridge from all that has gone before to going back out into a life of missionary witness and those additional forms of service to which the Spirit calls each one in their time and place.

The two disciples needed no explicit ritual to send them from the table back to Jerusalem. They had just experienced the restoration of their earlier calling to discipleship and having been sent on mission. That was powerful enough. For us today, the "rite of dismissal" from the table may seem too minimal and transitory to name and bear the weight of being that bridge to life-long mission. The late Cardinal Bernardin offers us an insightful mystagogical turn of phrase to help us see the dismissal differently. As we noted earlier, he writes: "The dismissal of the assembly is like the breaking of the bread. We have become 'the bread of life' and the 'cup of blessing' for the world. Now we are scattered, broken, poured out to be life for the world. What happens at home, at work, at meals? What do we make of our time, our words, our deeds, our resources of all kinds? That is what matters."[16]

Transformed with new awareness and resolve by the celebration of word and table, we are blessed and sent back into our lives of discipleship in the world, to take up our daily dying and rising with Christ, to be light to others, to serve them in love, to be his "silent witnesses" in the world.[17] The place of gathering then becomes the place of

16. Joseph Cardinal Bernardin, *Guide for the Assembly* (Chicago: Liturgy Training Publications, 1997), no. 79.

17. As noted earlier, the church documents on evangelization speak of "silent proclamation" by all the baptized as the first and absolutely non-

sending. Only a representative few leave the assembly in that final procession, but we should all know that we are marching out with them to take up our work and our lives of service, spreading God's love in the world.

From Mission to ?

That question can be answered in more than one way. For Gregory Pierce, mission is nothing less than "transforming the world."[18] That life task is unending and as large as the transformation the world itself awaits. Pierce offers an intriguing reversal of our ordinary perspective. He writes that the rite of dismissal, so brief and often uninspired, is in truth a vital part of the Eucharist. We gather for word and table precisely in order to be sent forth on mission. The mission work we then go out to resume is what we bring back to our next gathering. That act of gathering again, Pierce says, might better be thought of, not as just gathering, but as "return from mission."[19] The work to which we were sent on mission is brought into the assembly under the symbols of the cross we carry in to tell of our day-by-day giving of ourselves, the candles that are the light and warmth we shed in our world, and the book that tells the gospel story we are striving to live out. We return from mission to liturgy

---

negotiable requirement for the subsequent official activities of the church: missionary activity (explicit proclamation), initiatory activity (forming Christian communities), and pastoral activity (pastoral care of those communities). See *Ad Gentes* 11–12; *Evangelii Nuntiandi* 21; *Redemptoris Missio* 2–43; *General Directory for Catechesis* (Washington, DC: United States Catholic Conference, 1997), 47–49.

18. That is the subtitle of Gregory F. Augustine Pierce's book, *The Mass Is Never Ended: Rediscovering Our Mission to Transform the World* (Notre Dame, IN: Ave Maria Press, 2007).

19. Gregory Pierce, *The Mass Is Never Ended*, 43.

to be sent back out on mission in an ongoing cycle or, better, a spiral that links liturgy and life.[20]

At this point several paths may open up. Disciples on mission may have encountered other disciples already on the way for whom receiving the support of some form of ongoing ministry and formation is important. Or they may have found wavering disciples needing revitalization, or they may have identified potential new disciples who are searching, all walking a lonely path, dispirited and hungering for a companion to listen to their story and restore new hope and purpose to their lives. Mission would then initiate a new cycle of rewoven ministries, starting with companioning and listening to those who may be on their way to their own Emmaus.

From another perspective, the ministers themselves are deserving of pastoral care when they return from mission. Companioning them by walking with them, especially at moments set aside for reflective debriefing of their mission experience, would be important for their ongoing faith formation and development as disciples sent on mission.

In all these instances a new cycle of reweaving the entire pastoral ministry into an integrated approach would begin anew with listening together to discern how the Spirit of God is present and at work in their lives and mission.

Reweaving Strategies

The kind of questions Morris would have us ask[21] come from ministries of word and table. Have the homily, the

---

20. Karl Rahner speaks of life in the world as the "liturgy of the world," and Orthodox theologian Ion Bria speaks of it as "the liturgy after the liturgy." See Karl Rahner, "How to Receive a Sacrament and Mean It," *Theology Digest* 19 (1971): 227–34, and Ion Bria, "The Liturgy after the Liturgy," *International Review of Mission* 67, no. 265 (January 1978): 86–90.

21. Thomas H. Morris, "Liturgical Catechesis Revisited," *Catechumenate* 17, no. 3 (May 1994): 12–19, here at 16.

table sharing, the ritual actions, and the musical selections spoken not only convincingly of the risen Lord's presence with us at table but also irresistibly of his call to mission? And what pastoral strategies might we use to enhance and deepen awareness that the rite of dismissal is really a rite of sending us forth into mission?

It must be admitted at the outset that a rite so brief does not offer much possibility for elaboration. The structure of the rite is simple: a greeting, a blessing, and the dismissal. The gathering rite, in comparison, is embellished by a more formal procession using the symbols of cross, candles, and Gospel Book, accompanied by song. In the rite of dismissal, after the three structural elements just noted, the presider reverences the altar and "withdraws" (*recedit*). Withdrawal is a much less formal action than the actual "procession" used for the entrance,[22] and nothing is said about song. Common practice has supplied a semblance of "procession" with cross (book and candles sometimes), often with song. What are we to do?

Some favor keeping the rite as simple as possible—words of dismissal/sending with a strong mission thrust[23] and immediate departure by all participants, led by the presider or a deacon,[24] without an extended closing hymn. This would be a clearer response to the dismissal, that we are to immediately take the word proclaimed and the mystery of the cross just celebrated with us into daily life in the world. Others might welcome pastoral reflection on ways in which the sending might be elaborated ritually. Could the processional

22. Verbal description of the withdrawal (*recedit*) compared to the entrance procession (*introitus processione perficitur*) in the *General Instruction of the Roman Missal* 186 and 119.

23. The second and third options in the 2010 *Roman Missal* have that thrust, though it could be strengthened.

24. It would surely be fitting for a deacon (servant) to lead the assembly out into service in the world.

cross, candles, and Gospel Book used in the entrance rite be prominently featured in a dismissal procession as well? If the narthex is the place for gathering, is it not also the place for sending and then for return from mission? Could cross, candles, and Gospel Book be enshrined there at both gathering and sending, for people to venerate in both instances by touch or bow? Cross, candles, and Gospel Book symbolize what we each bring to the celebration and take back out into life. These tell the stories of what we are sent to live out.

Are there also ways we can appoint the narthex space itself for mission as well as for gathering, and can catechetical reflection help us see that the main door is the entryway both into the liturgical gathering and then into the liturgy of life to which we are sent?[25]

We also need to ask the mission question. How can the experience and wisdom garnered in the other ministries be brought into play? Surely those involved in the various ministries, both internal to the community and in outreach beyond, are an obvious resource to shape a community-wide awareness of available ministries and invite others to become coworkers.[26] Can that awareness also spur homilists to connect the day's readings with ways of offering to serve others in the name of Christ? Or challenge catechists and mystagogues to expand their catechetical ministry to include what Catherine Dooley calls "catechesis for

25. Some have suggested that placing words like "servant entrance" or "entry into service" above the inside of the main door might help keep us mindful of this connection. For other helpful mystagogical reflections on the dismissal, see Joyce Ann Zimmerman, "The Mystagogical Implications," in *A Commentary on the Order of Mass of the Roman Missal*, ed. Edward Foley (Collegeville, MN: Liturgical Press, 2011), 645–50.

26. Might representatives of the missions exercised by community members march out with the presider and deacon?

mission"?[27] And might that awareness of the fields ripe for mission not be a contribution those who companion folks and listen to their stories could make?

An example. A number of years ago I was doing a workshop for a large parish in a Midwestern city. I learned that the parish staff had established a very creative and inventive initiative for the Easter season. You may recall that the first reading for celebration of the Eucharist on each Sunday of Easter Time does not follow the normal pattern. It is taken, not from the first Testament, but from the Acts of the Apostles, which tell the story of ministry in the early church. During the Easter season every year the parish staff asks that all parishioners, in solidarity with the newly baptized who are then taking up some form of ministry, also commit themselves to some form of service for the coming year. It could be internal service of some kind for the parish itself, or it could be a form of social outreach to help address a larger issue in the area, for example, providing transportation to stores and medical appointments for shut-ins. When that year's commitment is completed, the next Easter season they are asked to make another one.

Strategies such as these are the stuff of reweaving the pastoral ministry into a collaborative effort of coworkers in the vineyard. As suggested at the end of chapter 2, that will require a vision of cultivating awareness across ministries, finding opportunities to enable effective communication and to foster collaboration between the ministries, and developing pastoral leadership committed to that vision and to cultivating it among the coworkers. Only thus can we reweave pastoral ministry.

---

27. Catherine Dooley, "To Be What We Celebrate: Engaging the Practice of Liturgical Catechesis," *New Theology Review* 17, no. 4 (November 2004): 9–17. She adds that phase to the standard three phases of liturgical catechesis—for, through, and from liturgy (14–16, here at 16).

A Final Reflection

The last four chapters have each concluded with the reflection that every ministry in its own way invites others into communion with Christ, their true companion and minister on the way. That is the final goal woven into all pastoral ministry. Disciples who minister, and indeed all disciples, are called to be sent, to serve others in his name, to be Christ to the world.[28]

28. Mark Searle, *Called to Participate: Theological, Ritual, and Social Perspectives*, ed. Barbara Searle and Anne Y. Koester (Collegeville, MN: Liturgical Press, 2006), 83, reports that "Pope John XXIII once remarked that Christians were the eighth sacrament and the only sacrament the nonbeliever could receive." See also "Christ has no body now but yours," a poem attributed to Teresa of Avila widely available on the web.

7

Reweaving the Ministries

This chapter will first revisit and gather up the fragments of the Emmaus narrative from the preceding chapters and reprise some of the earlier reflections on it. Second, we will reflect further on the world of the narrative.[1] Third, we will offer some considerations for pastoral practice today, to ask how the Emmaus narrative might be used in a community seeking to integrate and reweave the various local ministries at pivotal points in the life of the community.

The Emmaus Story Revisited

What better biblical paradigm is there for reweaving the ministries than the story of the two disciples on the way to Emmaus? If the breaking of the bread recounted in that Lukan narrative can be taken to have been the eucharistic rite, it deserves to be given pride of place as the first celebration of the Eucharist in the post-resurrection community, led by the risen Christ himself. As such, it deserves to remain paradigmatic for Christians of all times and places,

1. The first two sections are meant as a convenient resource for the facilitator conducting a reweaving workshop.

not only for celebration of the Eucharist, but also for the ministries within which the table scene is set. Historical distance has done little to diminish the story's impact; even today it is still a favorite among Christians, often taken as a model for various forms of ministry.[2]

The familiar account found in Luke 24:13-35, however, is not the only version of that journey. The longer ending of the Gospel of Mark contains a similar story (Mark 16:12-13). It reads:

> [12]After this he appeared in another form to two of them, as they were walking into the country. [13]And they went back and told the rest, but they did not believe them.

There is little in that brief matter-of-fact telling of the story to commend it to either imagination or memory. By contrast, the version contained in chapter 24 of the Gospel of Luke is a much more compelling story. It reads:

> [13]Now on that same day two of them were going to a village called Emmaus, about seven miles from Jerusalem,

2. For recent examples of that modeling, see Dominic F. Ashkar, *Road to Emmaus: A New Model for Catechesis* (San Jose, CA: Resource Publications, 1993); Stephen B. Bevans, "Introduction," in *Mission on the Road to Emmaus: Constants, Context and Prophetic Dialogue*, ed. Cathy Ross and Stephen B. Bevans, xi–xix (London: SCM, 2015); Regis A. Duffy, OFM, *An American Emmaus: Faith and Sacrament in the American Culture* (New York: Crossroad, 1995); Marcel Dumais, *After Emmaus: Biblical Models for the New Evangelization* (Collegeville, MN: Liturgical Press, 2014), 92–109; Thomas H. Groome, *Will There Be Faith? A New Vision for Educating and Growing Disciples* (New York: HarperOne, 2011), 39–44; Jeremy W. Langford, "Ministering to Gen-X Catholics, Jesus Style," *America* 183, no. 14 (April 22, 2000): 6–10; Timothy Radcliffe, "Introduction," in *A Handbook for Catholic Preaching*, ed. Edward Foley, xiv–xxi (Collegeville, MN: Liturgical Press, 2016); Ann O'Shea, "The Emmaus Story: A Model for Pastoral Supervision," *Journal of Supervision and Training in Ministry* 9 (1987): 29–34.

[14]and talking with each other about all these things that had happened. [15]While they were talking and discussing, Jesus himself came near and went with them, [16]but their eyes were kept from recognizing him. [17]And he said to them, "What are you discussing with each other while you walk along?" They stood still, looking sad. [18]Then one of them, whose name was Cleopas, answered him, "Are you the only stranger in Jerusalem who does not know the things that have taken place there in these days?" [19]He asked them, "What things?" They replied, "The things about Jesus of Nazareth, who was a prophet mighty in deed and word before God and all the people, [20]and how our chief priests and leaders handed him over to be condemned to death and crucified him. [21]But we had hoped that he was the one to redeem Israel. Yes, and besides all this, it is now the third day since these things took place. [22]Moreover, some women of our group astounded us. They were at the tomb early this morning, [23]and when they did not find his body there, they came back and told us that they had indeed seen a vision of angels who said that he was alive. [24]Some of those who were with us went to the tomb and found it just as the women had said, but they did not see him." [25]Then he said to them, "Oh, how foolish you are, and how slow of heart to believe all that the prophets have declared! [26]Was it not necessary that the Messiah should suffer these things and then enter into his glory?" [27]Then beginning with Moses and all the prophets, he interpreted to them the things about himself in all the scriptures.

[28]As they came near the village to which they were going, he walked ahead as if he were going on. [29]But they urged him strongly, saying, "Stay with us, because it is almost evening and the day is now nearly over." So he went in to stay with them. [30]When he was at the table with them, he took bread, blessed and broke it, and gave it to them. [31]Then their eyes were opened, and they recognized him; and he vanished from their sight. [32]They

said to each other, "Were not our hearts burning within us while he was talking to us on the road, while he was opening up the scriptures to us?" [33]That same hour they got up and returned to Jerusalem; and they found the eleven and their companions gathered together. [34]They were saying, "The Lord has risen indeed, and he has appeared to Simon!" [35]Then they told what had happened on the road, and how he had been made known to them in the breaking of the bread.

The World of the Narrative

Luke's version of the story of the two disciples is superbly crafted. It not only fleshes out the details of the episode and gives it a different ending but also provides the hearer with many points of entry into the inner experience of the disciples' journey. If outer events are the envelope that contains and expresses the inner flow of experience, the contemporary reader might want to go back over the account at this point with underlining pencil in hand and with questions such as these in mind. In the flow of events and conversation, what are the significant moments and turning points in the story? What words or phrases resonate even now to reveal the inner journey that is unfolding? The following reflective commentary offers one way of interpreting that journey.[3]

The opening verses (24:13-14) set the scene. Two disciples are on their way to Emmaus. The road they travel is to be measured not just by the physical distance of "seven miles." As is often the case with the stories we tell, prepositions often mark significant turning points. The journey they are making is not just a journey "*to* the village called Emmaus" and *to*

---

3. What follows was initially inspired by Denis McBride, *The Gospel of Luke: A Reflective Commentary* (Northport, NY: Costello, 1982), 317–18. See also the more extended reflective commentary by Eugene LaVerdiere, *Dining in the Kingdom of God: The Origins of the Eucharist according to Luke* (Chicago, IL: Liturgy Training Publications, 1994), 153–74.

what a different future will now hold for them but one *"from*
Jerusalem" and *from* the past they are leaving behind—perhaps even fleeing from—including the band of the disciples
of Jesus and "all those things that had happened" there (v.
14). The full inner meaning of that flight from Jerusalem will
become clearer in the course of the account.

As the first scene unfolds (vv. 15-24), the Jesus they once
followed joins them on their journey (v. 15), now a stranger
to their eyes (v. 16). The disciples are engaged in a lively
exchange (v. 15) that consumes them and leaves them on
the edge of deep "distress"[4] (v. 17). The stranger's gentle
questions, "What are you discussing?" (v. 17) and "What
things?" (v. 19), reopen the floodgates, and the whole story
they had been discussing comes cascading out once again.
It is the story of all "the things that have taken place there
in these days" (v. 18). It recounts in simple detail the first
part of the kerygma, up to the death of Jesus, but there it
ends abruptly without the final ending that Jesus rose and
is "the Lord." The ending of the story they tell is a bitter
one: "We had hoped . . ." (v. 21). It is a story of deep disillusionment and shattered hopes.

But what were those lost hopes? The text says they had
hoped "that he was the one to redeem Israel" (v. 21). These
words deserve a further exploration. An earlier passage in
Luke offers us a clue when it gives voice to what the disciples were anticipating as Jesus and his band approached
Jerusalem for the last time (Luke 19:11). There we read:

> As they were listening to this, he went on to tell a parable
> [the departing nobleman who entrusted various sums of
> money to ten servants], because he was near Jerusalem,
> and because *they supposed that the kingdom of God was to
> appear immediately.* (emphasis added)

---

4. The Greek word *skythrōpos*, translated as "looking sad," can also
mean looking gloomy, grim-faced, dejected.

Two things help to situate those hopes historically. First, "these days" (24:18) during which those events had taken place were Passover week. Passover was a pilgrimage feast for which the all Israelites gathered in Jerusalem to keep the memory of the great deeds by which God had led them out of slavery and made a covenant with them. Scripture scholars have taught us that, in the vocabulary of that time, "to remember" is more than simply recollecting that something happened in the past. Moses instructed a new generation of wanderers in the desert: "The LORD our God made a covenant with us at Horeb. Not with our ancestors did the LORD make this covenant, but with us, who are all of us here alive today" (Deut 5:2-3). In the moment of ritual remembering, past events become real events to those who keep their memory. Events that become real in the remembering demand, in turn, not simply a recollection of past ancestral response to the God who acts to save but a fresh response to be made here and now. The people gathered in Jerusalem for Passover each year in order to keep covenant, or, better, to respond anew and *make* covenant in the fullest sense of the word. It was for the Passover feast that Jesus and his band made their way to Jerusalem, to join with all the people in remembering the covenant.

Second, as commentators tell us, that period of Jewish history was a time of heightened messianic expectations. It was a time of widespread hope that the new, interior covenant of which the prophets had dreamed (Jer 31:31-33) would come to pass and that the lasting reign of God it would usher in was near at hand.[5] From the very beginning, the ministry of Jesus centered on his announcement that the reign of God was about to appear. His growing sense of urgency about the nearness of God's reign and his role in bringing it about are clear enough in both his Galilean min-

---

5. In the context of the Roman occupation and rule, this was easily interpreted in a political sense. Jesus believed otherwise.

istry (Luke 4:14–9:50) and the second phase of his ministry in Luke's account, the long teaching journey to Jerusalem (Luke 9:51–19:27). Recall his words about the ripening harvest and his strategy of extending his own ministry by sending first the Twelve (Luke 9:1-6, 10) in the Galilean phase, and then additional messengers (Luke 9:52-53), and finally the seventy in the second phase (Luke 10:1-12, 17-20). Their mission, like his, was to announce the coming of God's reign by word, by expelling demons, and by healing the sick.

The mixed success with which the message of the coming of God's reign was received, both in the Galilean phase and on the journey to Jerusalem, only heightened that sense of urgency. To finally accomplish that mission, what better time and place could there have been than Passover week when all the people, filled with great messianic hopes, were gathered in Jerusalem to keep/make covenant? The disciples had gone with Jesus to Jerusalem where, they supposed, "the kingdom of God was to appear immediately." They had gone to the feast with Jesus to remember the covenant, in high hopes that he would be the one to finally "redeem Israel" (24:21).

Against that backdrop, the story the two had to tell as they made their way from Jerusalem to Emmaus was one of bitter disillusionment and lost hope. As Denis McBride notes, their story is told in the past tense. To tell the story in that way means that it has ended in failure: "we had hoped that he was the one to redeem Israel" (v. 21). The exhilarating hopes they had brought to Jerusalem have completely vanished. Telling the story in the past tense also reveals their shattered sense of themselves. What they are saying about themselves is this: "they are ex-followers of a prophet, with left-over lives, and nowhere to go but away."[6] What else was there for them to do but flee, abandoning

---

6. McBride, *The Gospel of Luke*, 317–18.

both their dead leader and his band of followers?[7] That's what we do when life feels that way. At the gentle invitation of the stranger who listens so well, the truth of their experience has now been told, and it has been heard with empathy and respect.

That pained admission of disillusionment and lost hope immediately leads into the next scene in Luke's narrative (vv. 25-27). When the two have exhausted their story, the stranger replies: "Oh, how foolish you are, and how slow of heart to believe all that the prophets have declared!" (v. 25). He then proceeds to retell the very same story, "beginning with Moses and all the prophets" (v. 27). His version ends, however, not in failure, but in triumph: "Was it not necessary that the Messiah should suffer these things and then enter into his glory?" (v. 26).

There is a sheer mastery in the stranger's retelling of their story. The experience that is recounted is theirs. The words of the retelling are also theirs, familiar words borrowed from Moses and the prophets. Through these, "he interpreted to them the things about himself in all the scriptures" (v. 27). But what is new is how the familiar words are now broken open to take on an unforeseen meaning, to bear and name in a new way not only the past experience of their people but also what they themselves had experienced. That is biblical "interpreting" (v. 27) or "opening up" (v. 32) the scriptures at its best. Though they would only put it into words later, when they could name the "burning" of their hearts (v. 32), the impact of such storytelling is predictable, as is also its sequel. At the stranger's invitation they had told their story, and in response he has accepted their version of the story and has given them that same story to retell, but with a new ending. He has hosted their hurts and re-

---

7. At the end of the garden scene Mark's Gospel starkly notes: "All of them deserted him and fled" (Mark 14:50).

stored their hopes. The cycle of gratitude and hospitality ought not be broken: "Stay with us, because it is almost evening and the day is now nearly over" (v. 29). "So he went in to stay with them"[8] (v. 29).

As the narrative shifts from the journey to the table scene (vv. 28-31), the stranger who entered the room as guest becomes the host and leads them in the table ritual over the bread (v. 30). And in that moment the disciples' journey reaches completion: "their eyes were opened, and they recognized him" (v. 31). They had left Jerusalem with no further hopes for the coming of God's reign and their part in bringing it about and with shattered faith in a Jesus now laid in a tomb. At best, their faith had never been more than that "little faith" for which Jesus had so often chided them, a faith still only as tiny as a mustard seed (Matt 17:20; Luke 17:6). And even that little faith had been shattered by the events of those past few days. Now, however, in the moment of the breaking of the bread they have recognized him in the stranger. In the evening dusk of that day Easter faith has dawned for them.

In the appearance accounts, it should be noted, recognition of the risen Jesus is never simply a physical recognition that the Jesus of Nazareth whom they had known is still alive. Rather, the one who appears to the disciples is recognized in faith, not simply as the Jesus of Nazareth they had once known, but as "the Lord" (see John 21:7). That moment of recognition is not physical sight but "faith insight."[9] The two

---

8. This moment is beautifully captured in a bas-relief in the pilgrims' cloister ambulatory in Santo Domingo de Silos in Spain. It shows the stranger doing a crossover dance step in response to their invitation to stay.

9. See Raymond E. Brown, *The Virginal Conception and Bodily Resurrection of Jesus* (New York: Paulist Press, 1973), 111–14. The "eyes kept from recognizing him" (Luke 24:16), symbolic of their being "slow of heart to believe" (v. 25), are now "opened" in full belief "and they recognized him" (v. 31).

disciples reached the destination of their journey when their eyes were opened in recognition at the Emmaus table (Luke 24:31). They have made their way from that "little faith" that was shattered in Jerusalem to a full Easter faith, from loss of hope to hope reborn. In that moment, they have come not only to recognize him as the Lord risen and alive but also to know themselves once again as believing disciples, as disciples to whom he had given a mission that endures. They are once more on the way, not to Emmaus, but to following the one who had once told them, "I am the way" (John 14:6).[10]

With that, Luke's account moves rapidly to a close with two final scenes (vv. 32 and 33-35). In the light of their new-found faith and mission, the two disciples are now able to put into words how the stranger's story had set their "hearts burning"[11] on the way (Luke 24:32). And empowered and impelled by what they had experienced, they "got up and returned to Jerusalem" (v. 33), to give witness to the others of "what had happened on the road, and how he had been made known to them in the breaking of the bread" (v. 35).

It is clear enough that the journey of the two disciples from Jerusalem to Emmaus has been a journey from loss of hope and faith in Jesus to full Easter faith and revival of their hopes, their sense of being disciples again and still having a mission. In Luke's hands a simple appearance account has been expanded into five finely detailed scenes and fashioned

10. The word Jesus used was *hodos* (road/way). The two disciples' account of "what had happened on the road [*hodos*]" uses the same Greek word in Luke 24:35, translated as "the way" in the New American Bible, Revised Edition. Followers of "the way" (*hodos*) was the earliest name for Christians (Acts 9:2). This is a delightful play on words to name the inner journey of the disciples—going a-way and returning to "the way" because of what happened "on the way"—expressed also as their eyes being "kept" and "opened" (Luke 24:16 and 31).

11. In a lovely phrase, theologian-poet John Shea names the stranger the "arsonist of the heart," in his *The Hour of the Unexpected* (Niles, IL: Argus Communications, 1977), 49.

into a journey story that still has the power to capture in a paradigmatic way something of the inner path by which believers have always come to faith. But the story is paradigmatic in more ways than that. It also embodies within it a much larger and more integrated vision of pastoral ministry than we are accustomed to harbor. Can there be a more fruitful or better biblical paradigm than the Emmaus story to model for us a renewed vision for reweaving all pastoral ministry? That is the paradigm this book has explored, a paradigm that can serve us well as we work to reweave the ministries. To that reweaving we now return.

Pastoral Considerations for the Reweaving

Each of the five preceding chapters has ended with a section on strategies for reweaving the ministries. Here we will look first at several scenarios in which the Emmaus narrative might be used to integrate and reweave the various local ministries at pivotal points in the life of the community. After that we will highlight some guiding principles for that pastoral practice.

Reweaving Scenarios

When might reweaving the ministries be called for in a community? Some of the most frequent occasions for attending to inter-ministry collaboration would be those transitional times that recur annually in the liturgical calendar. There are five seasons in the liturgical year: Advent and Christmas Times, linked by the celebration of Christmas; Lent and Easter Times, linked by the celebration of the Paschal Triduum and concluding with Pentecost; and Ordinary Time,[12] which is broken into segments interspersed before and after the other seasons.

---

12. A better title, following the Latin original, would be "Time throughout the Year" (*Tempus per Annum*) or "Season of the Year." That period is

In preparation and planning for these changes of liturgical seasons, there are several questions the various ministries can be asked to reflect on, first separately and then together.

The first questions have to do with the experience of people:

> *How do the experience, activities, and expectations of life in the two seasons differ?*

> *What shift of moods and feelings (joy, sadness) does this transition evoke in people?*

> *What influential factors are there in the surrounding culture, local traditions, weather?*

The questions then turn to the task of interweaving the ministries:

> *Are there common "story lines" that require affirmation or special pastoral attention?*

> *Can those stories be put into conversation with the biblical stories of the next season's lectionary?*

> *Which ministry/ministries take the lead in addressing the responses to those questions?*

> *How can the other ministries contribute and support?*

The next questions concern details of the pastoral response:

---

not simply "ordinary" calendar time, but rather the arena for *kairos* time, the time of salvation in which the entire life and ministry of Christ are remembered, proclaimed, and celebrated. It is a time for disciples to grow more fully, day by day, into living the mystery of Christ "in all its aspects" (*General Norms for the Liturgical Year and the Calendar* 43).

What is to be the pastoral response?

What core actions, events, and channels of communication are needed?

To whom are their planning and implementation entrusted?

Are any special resources needed?

Since this scenario is concerned primarily with the liturgical life of the community, there are obvious choices about which ministries would normally have a leading role. First, liturgical ministry (including liturgical planners, environment planners, musicians, ministers, homilists, and presiders) would play a primary role. Second, catechetical ministry would also have a major role in seasons that involve celebration of first sacraments and the rites in the RCIA. Because of the integral connection between liturgical and mystagogical catechesis,[13] catechetical ministry would also have a continuing role in the liturgical life of the community in all the seasons.

There are a number of basic resources regarding the liturgical seasons, including official documents,[14] pastoral commentaries on them,[15] and liturgical-theological commentaries on the seasons. Especially helpful for both liturgical and catechetical ministries is a three-volume commentary by

13. See chapters 3 and 5 above, as well as appendixes 1 and 2 below.

14. Roman documents include: SC 102–21, on liturgical year and music; "The Cycle of the Year," in *Universal Norms on the Liturgical Year and the Calendar*, nos. 17–44 (approved by Paul VI, 1969), found in the *Roman Missal* (ICEL translation, 2010), 110–15. USCCB documents include: *Music in Catholic Worship* (1972, 1983); *Liturgical Music Today* (1982).

15. See, for example, the commentaries in *The Liturgy Documents: A Parish Resource*, 2 vols. (Chicago, IL: Liturgy Training Publications, 1991/2012 and 1999/2014).

Dianne Bergant, *Preaching the New Lectionary*.[16] At the beginning of each season/segment (Ordinary Time is divided into four segments), there are charts laying out the flow and connections of biblical readings for that season/segment, situating them in their liturgical context. This is especially helpful in answering the work of putting peoples' common life stories in conversation with the season's biblical stories already determined in the season's lectionary.

Other regularly recurring transitions might be those between summertime and the rest of the year (spring-summer-fall-winter). These transitions involve the changing of seasons and alternations between work, school, and vacation. These not only involve changes in how we experience life as a whole but also impact what goes on in the community's liturgical life and ministry.

Finally, other occasions for asking how to effectively integrate the ministries might be important junctures such as a pandemic, catastrophes such as floods and hurricanes, important parish anniversaries, sudden major shifts/divisions in community demographics, merging of parishes, etc. Questions for pastoral reflection on these changes by the ministries, separately and together, would be similar to those above. The pattern could follow the Emmaus paradigm: walking with people and listening to their experience and the stories they share; looking for ways to bring these stories into conversation with pertinent biblical stories; moving that conversation into appropriate forms of prayerful lament, petition, and praise before God; and finally, finding practical ways to respond to the situation.

In all three scenarios, the Emmaus story might be suitable for use in inter-ministry gatherings to address the situation

16. Dianne Bergant with Richard Fragomeni, *Preaching the New Lectionary*, 3 vols. (Collegeville, MN: Liturgical Press, Year A 2001, Year B 1999, Year C 2000).

at hand. It could surely model an understanding of how to collaborate and interweave those ministries. In some cases it might also serve as the biblical story to partner with the life stories of the people in the conversation. If the pastoral response to the situation requires a more protracted process, the Emmaus narrative could serve as the centerpiece in a workshop situated in the middle of that longer process, between the first two phases and the last three of the Emmaus story. A description of such an actual workshop is given in appendix 4.

Some Guiding Principles

We will now gather up some of the more important general principles to guide a local community in reweaving the ministries into an integrated pastoral practice to effectively address scenarios such as those.[17]

- *A vision of integrated pastoral ministry.*
  This is best developed and adopted officially by community leadership, always in collaboration with those in the various ministries who have more personal and direct access to the difficulties and concerns in the lives of the people they serve.

- *Commitment to take appropriate steps to implement the vision.*
  Community leadership needs to do everything necessary to elicit wide buy-in by leaders of the ministries and all those who work in those ministries. That is why widespread participation in arriving at the vision is important. A vision without such commitment and acceptance is at risk of remaining unfulfilled.

---

17. See also the sections on reweaving strategies at the end of the earlier chapters, especially chapter 2.

- *Structures to enable and coordinate the implementation.*
  Such structures include periodic staff meetings of the
  community leadership for reports from and oversight
  of the ministries and regular meetings of the individual ministries with their particular leaders to over-
  see and manage the details of the work in their area
  of ministry.

- *Enlistment and appropriate preparation/formation of
  workers for and in the ministries.*
  Personal interest and gifts for the particular work of a
  ministry are obvious starting points for discernment
  on the part of applicants and leaders of the individual
  ministry. To facilitate the discernment there would
  normally be a job description of the expectations and
  tasks of the applicant's role to facilitate the discernment. Preparation would normally include some form
  of apprenticeship under an experienced member of
  the ministry, coupled with an effective formation in
  the theological-spiritual underpinnings of this particular ministry.[18] This formation would help the new
  members of a ministry to understand the overarching
  vision of the community, to see their particular role as
  part of the larger pastoral ministry of the community,
  and to accept the need to be concerned and active not
  only in their specialty but in the entire ministry of the
  community. Only thus can disciples come to lead and
  carry out their several ministries as true coworkers.

This last guiding principle is probably as crucial as the
first one. The vision for weaving all the ministries together

---

18. For a detailed approach to forming coworkers for inter-ministry
collaboration, see Jane E. Regan, *Where Two or Three Are Gathered: Transforming the Parish through Communities of Practice* (New York: Paulist Press,
2016), 27–46.

into an integrated whole will not succeed if the individual ministers do not endorse it and share the passion and commitment to be coworkers in the vineyard. To bolster that understanding, in an article titled "Toward a Fundamental Theology of Ministry" Kathleen Cahalan offers some strong convictions worth quoting at length:

> Ministers can overly identify with one practice of ministry because they are hired for a particular role in a particular context. A catechist, pastoral counselor, or school administrator may come to view their particular practice as so pre-eminent it becomes disconnected from the other practices over time. Because the role and setting strongly determine the ministry, ministers may fail to see the ways in which catechetical ministry or pastoral care encompasses all aspects of ministry, not just specialization in a particular area. In other words, to what extent does the catechist understand his or her ministry to include pastoral care with parishioners or students, and when does the pastoral counselor take time to catechize a hospital patient and family? Further, how does the liturgist play a role in catechizing the parish and how is preaching related to prophecy and the administration of the community's resources?[19]

> Every minister meets the disciple as disciple—not some part of discipleship. . . . Each minister strives to embody all aspects of ministry in their work because they meet the disciple as disciple. Likewise, ministers are called to serve in relationship to the whole of ministry in whatever setting or role they assume: the liturgist is also catechist, the pastoral counselor is also prophet, and the administrator is able to lead the community in prayer.[20]

---

19. Kathleen A. Cahalan, "Toward a Fundamental Theology of Ministry," *Worship* 80, no. 2 (March 2006): 102-120, at 107.
20. Cahalan, "Toward a Fundamental Theology," 119.

A bit later she continues:

> Specialization is well suited for the ministers' charisms and the community's good. But that specialized role is never separate from the minister's responsibility to participate in a community in which all aspects of ministry are present. Likewise, in areas where an individual minister is not as well equipped or capable, they work in tandem with others to insure that disciples are well served.[21]

A Final Image to Ponder

In a reception area of the school where I teach hangs an artwork that Robert Silvers produced for the Jesus 2000 competition. This huge Photomosaic[22] is a collage of small individual pieces, a modern version of mosaics. When viewed close up, the individual pieces can be identified as photographs of fragments of scrolls (Dead Sea and others). The texts are written against variously hued backgrounds. Seen from farther away, the image of a human face emerges from the hues. Silvers titled the work "The Word Became Flesh"—an amazing artistic fusing of words and the Word of God who speaks the words of God.

Silvers's artwork reminds me of something Karl Rahner has written, that only in Jesus did God's Word become flesh. But that means, Rahner says, that any human could have become the Incarnate Word; that possibility is part and parcel of human nature. To be human, Rahner says, is to be "the grammar of a possible self-utterance of God."[23] We are

---

21. Cahalan, "Toward a Fundamental Theology," 120.

22. Photomosaic, a term copyrighted by Silvers, combines small individual photographic pieces by computer to replicate an overall image. This work is about six feet high by five feet wide.

23. Karl Rahner, "On the Theology of the Incarnation," in *Theological Investigations* 4, trans. Kevin Smyth (Baltimore, MD: Helicon, 1996), 105–20, here at 115.

not the Word Incarnate, but as his disciples we can each in our own way become a small word of God, if we echo to others something of the Word Incarnate. We are like the pieces of his image, together forming for our world a mosaic of the one who is truly the Word of God. This is not just a superficial relationship; we can say with Paul that we, though many, are one body, baptized into the Body of Christ (1 Cor 12:12-13), "always carrying in the body the death of Jesus, so that the life of Jesus may also be made visible in our bodies" (2 Cor 4:10). Provided we echo to others the word of total love God spoke to our world in the life and death of Jesus.

All those in pastoral ministry, "disciples who become leaders in the community,"[24] are coworker stand-ins for the risen Lord. They are the guise the stranger now wears to accompany and minister to disciples on the way, to walk with them, and to send them to speak and act in his name. How, then, can the ministries be fitted together as a grand mosaic of Christ? Or in the image running throughout this book, how can those ministries be rewoven into a grand tapestry of that image? That reweaving is what we have been reflecting on in this book.

---

24. This "broad definition of ministry" comes from Cahalan, "Toward a Fundamental Theology," 116.

Appendixes

These appendixes will provide interested readers some further notes on catechesis, mystagogy, and the relation between mission and ministry, as well as a description of how the Emmaus account was actually used in a workshop for reweaving parish ministries.

1 Technical Note on Catechesis

Catechesis comes from two Greek words, "down" (*katá*) and "sound" (*ēkhḗ*), combined to form the verb "to sound down" (*katēkhéō*), literally "to echo." It is usually translated as "to instruct orally." In the Christian context, as the *General Directory for Catechesis* notes, "catechesis is nothing other than the process of transmitting the Gospel, as the Christian community has received it, understands it, celebrates it, lives it and communicates it in many ways."[1] As oral instruction, catechesis is a form of ministry of the word. Ministry of the word, in turn, is part of the overall mission of the church to evangelize, that is, to spread the Gospel (GDC 46–57, 60–72).

The Gospel, however, should not be understood narrowly as only words. In the Gospel it is the Word of God who speaks words of God (John 3:34), but he also does the saving works his Abba gave him to do (see John 5:36; 17:4). *Dei*

---

1. Congregation for the Clergy, *General Directory for Catechesis* (Washington, DC: United States Conference, 1998), 105; hereafter GDC in text.

Verbum has stated that Jesus fulfills revelation "through his whole work of making himself present and manifesting himself: through His words and deeds, His signs and wonders, but especially through His death and glorious resurrection from the dead and final sending of the Spirit of truth."[2] In a word, Jesus is revelation in all he says, does, and is. In effect, the Gospel is Jesus, "the way, the truth, and the life. No one comes to the Father except through me" (John 14:6). It follows that "at the heart of catechesis we find, in essence, a Person, the Person of Jesus of Nazareth . . . who suffered and died for us and who now after rising, is living with us forever. It is Jesus who is 'the way and the truth, and the life,' and Christian living consists in following Christ, in the *sequela Christi*."[3]

Accordingly, "the definitive aim of catechesis is to put people not only in touch, but also in communion and intimacy, with Jesus Christ; only he can lead us to the love of the Father in the Spirit and make us share in the life of the Holy Trinity" (CT 5; GDC 80). Catechesis has to do with forming disciples for the journey. "All catechesis should provide those being catechized with the opportunity to journey with Christ through the stages of his Paschal Mystery."[4] Journeying with Christ calls for an ongoing process of formation for growth in conversion and faith (GDC 56).

We will return to this theme of ongoing catechetical formation in the next note on mystagogy. Here it suffices to say that all catechesis, taking its inspiration from the bap-

2. Vatican II, Dogmatic Constitution on Divine Revelation, *Dei Verbum* 5 (1965), hereafter DV in text.

3. John Paul II, On Catechesis for Our Time, *Catechesi Tradendae* 5 (1979), hereafter CT in text.

4. United States Conference of Catholic Bishops, *National Directory for Catechesis* (Washington, DC: USCCB, 2005), 116.

tismal catechumenate (GDC 90–91), needs to be characterized by a comprehensiveness and integrity of formation (GDC 90–92), modeled in the RCIA as an apprenticeship in believing, praying, community, and service (see RCIA 76). All catechesis deals more with an integrated following of Jesus' way than with just knowing about it.

2 Technical Note on Mystagogy

Following up on the previous note on catechesis, we now look at mystagogy in greater depth. In the late second century, Christians borrowed this word from contemporary mystery religions. The word "mystagogy" comes from two Greek roots, "mystery" (*mustḗrion*), derived from the verb "to close/shut [one's eyes or mouth]" (*múein*) and the verb "to lead/guide" (*ágein*). A mystagogue (*mystagōgos*) is an experienced guide who leads an initiate into the mystery. In the early catechumenate mystagogy was a form of catechesis that usually came after the reception of the sacraments of initiation. The mystagogue, normally the bishop, led the newly baptized in a week-long series of reflections on what they had experienced at their initiation. He led them through the rites of initiation, moment by moment. He evoked images, metaphors, and stories from the Scriptures that he interpreted spiritually to help the newly baptized to understand more deeply the mystery celebrated in the rites and symbols of initiation. Mystagogy was usually the final phase of the ancient catechumenate.

Today mystagogy is also the name given to the final period of the catechumenate, when the newly baptized are fully inserted into the community and continue their formation in faith and Christian living (RCIA 244–47). Three subtle differences from classical mystagogy are worth noting.

First, in current documents of the church mystagogy is broader in scope, and other names are used for it. For these documents faith formation does not end with the RCIA. The complete span of the church's evangelizing activity begins with lived witness (silent proclamation) and progresses through missionary activity (explicit proclamation), initiatory activity (founding communities, especially through RCIA), and pastoral activity (ongoing pastoral care of those communities). The work of mystagogy takes place in the last phase of the RCIA, but it continues beyond it under the names of "continuing catechesis," "permanent catechesis," "permanent formation," and "continuing formation in faith." "In a broader sense, mystagogy represents the Christian's lifelong education and formation in the faith" (NDC 117; see also CT 70; GDC 51, 69–72).

Second, the scope of that continuing formation extends beyond a mystagogy of the rites of initiation to include Scripture study, Christian reading of events, liturgical catechesis, catechesis about circumstances of personal, family, ecclesial, or social life, and theological instruction—all to be linked together in harmonious complementarity (GDC 71–72). It addresses the totality of Christian life.

Third, in keeping with current developments in educational theory and methods, greater attention is to be paid to the local socio-cultural contexts, experience, and to active participation of people (GDC 52, 173–74; NDC 97–98).[1]

One final note. Like the classical catechumenate, the impact of initiatory catechesis today is not meant to cease after the period of mystagogy. The aim of all catechesis is forming Christians for living out the values of God's reign in a mission of silent proclamation of the Gospel. Thus, to the standard three phases of liturgical catechesis—*for, through,* and *from* liturgy—Catherine Dooley adds the fourth phase of

---

1. The mystagogy of the classical catechumenate was more narrowly focused on the liturgy and was entrusted to the mystagogue who provided the mystagogical interpretation. *Dei Verbum* 8 now affirms an active role of the faithful in the "growth in the understanding of the realities and the words which have been handed down . . . through a penetrating understanding of the spiritual realities which they experience."

"catechesis for mission."[2] That addition should hold true
for all catechesis.

In a sense, the stranger's ministry of the word addressed
in chapter 3 falls under this broader understanding of mystagogy, for the two disciples had already received a first
catechesis during the time of their previous following of
Jesus; they now receive a continuing catechesis about who
he is and about the mission he had entrusted to them.[3]
They will be able to name that continuing catechesis at the
supper scene in Emmaus.

This broader understanding of mystagogy as ongoing
formation is being used in this book.

2. Catherine Dooley, "To Be What We Celebrate: Engaging the Practice
of Liturgical Catechesis," *New Theology Review* 17, no. 4 (November 2004):
14–16.

3. GDC 51, footnote 64, cites John Paul II's distinction between "basic
formation and permanent formation."

3 Theological Notes on Mission and Ministry

This note reflects on mission and ministry and how they are connected. The Vatican II Decree on the Apostolate of the Laity offers a starting point when it states that "in the church there is a diversity of ministry but oneness of mission."[1] This implies that mission and ministry are related but not identical. Mission is broader and ties the diverse ministries together,[2] so that is our starting premise.

As we noted earlier, the word "mission" means sending, and Jesus chose to describe himself as one sent.[3] His mission was to spread to all the ends of the earth the "fountain-like love" of God from which mission flows (AG 2–4).[4] In fulfillment of that mission, Jesus came, "not to be served, but to serve and to give his life as a ransom for many" (AG 3, quoting Mark 10:45). That is how he identified himself. His mission was one of service. To his disciples arguing at the Last Supper about who should be regarded as the greatest, Jesus pointed to his own example. Unlike the kings of the Gentiles

1. Vatican II, Decree on the Apostolate of the Laity, *Apostolicam Actuositatem* 2 (1965), http://www.vatican.va/archive/hist_councils/ii_vatican _council/documents/vat-ii_decree_19651118_apostolicam-actuositatem _en.html. Hereafter cited in text as AA.

2. *Missio Dei* is commonly seen today as the broader, overarching reality, with particular ministries falling within it. For a differing view, see Titus Presler, "Mission Is Ministry in the Dimension of Difference: A Definition for the Twenty-first Century," *International Bulletin of Missionary Research* 34, no. 4 (October 2010): 195–204.

3. "Mission" comes from *mittere* (to send), the Latin translation of *apostéllein*.

4. This appended note uses some elements from the Vatican II principles on mission found in *Ad Gentes* 2–5, 11–12. Hereafter cited in text as AG.

who lord it over their people, he said "I am among you as one who serves [*diákonōn*]" (Luke 22:27). In washing the feet of his disciples, he showed that same menial attitude.[5] That is the attitude of service Jesus required of the disciples he sent to continue his mission: "I have set you an example, that you also should do as I have done to you" (John 13:12-16). They are not to be called teacher/master; even the greatest among them should be their servant/minister (*diákonos*; Matt 23:8-11).[6] Service/ministry was to be the hallmark of their mission, as it was for Jesus.

In carrying on the mission of Jesus, the church "must walk the road Christ himself walked, a path of poverty and obedience, of service and self-sacrifice even to death" (AG 5). The baptized are to walk in this same way of self-giving service in love. The fundamental life task/mission of all disciples is to give silent witness to God's unselfish love (AG 11–12); mission is to be done in the mode of service. Service is at the heart of mission.

This language of service brings us to the question of what ministry is and how it relates to mission. The word "ministry" derives from the Latin verb *ministrare*, "to serve, attend, wait upon."[7] A minster is literally a "lesser one," one who serves.[8] The Greek equivalent, *diákonos*, has that same

5. An early Christian hymn names his underlying attitude even more strongly: "taking the form of a slave [*doúlou*]" (Phil 2:7).

6. There is a delightful play on words here. Just as minister derives from *min(us)+ister* in Latin, the little one, so master derives from *magister*, a compound of *mag(nus)+ister*, the great one, with authority and power.

7. *Ministrare* derives in turn from the Latin adjective *minus* (neuter form of *minor*), the comparative form of *parvus* ("small, little").

8. Somewhat ironically, current practice also uses "minister" for one who "serves" in a position of authority, such as members of the government, e.g., as a minister of defense or a foreign minister, a political leader, church leaders, or leaders of a religious congregation. In such cases, unlike the typical New Testament usage, "servant" can also take on connotations of authority and power.

meaning for Christians in the New Testament. The language of service/ministry (*diakonía*) abounds in the early church. Various forms of service are recorded, though not always named in that way.

Several features are pertinent here. First, although there is a wide variety of gifts of the Spirit, there is close unity among them. They all come from the same source: spiritual gifts from the Spirit, forms of service from the Lord, and workings from God (1 Cor 12:4-6). They are all given for a single purpose. "To each one is given the manifestation of the Spirit for the common good" (1 Cor 12:7). Disciples called to each ministry are to "equip all the saints [the people of God] for the work of ministry [*diakonía*], for building up the body of Christ" (Eph 4:12).

Second, within that variety of services, Paul singles out several ministerial roles that seem to be commonly known (1 Cor 12:8-10, 28; Eph 4:11). Among the earliest ministries to emerge in the early church were ministry of the word (Acts 6:4) and the practical ministry of serving at table (Acts 6:2). But other "forms of assistance" (1 Cor 12:28), like the relief collection for the Jerusalem community (Acts 11:29; 1 Cor 16:1; 2 Cor 9:12-13), surfaced in response to the rise of particular needs.

Third, using a human analogy, Paul writes that different gifts of ministry are like parts of the body. None can say they do not belong to the body or that they have no need of the others (1 Cor 12:1-21). They must all work together "to equip the saints for the work of ministry [*diakonías*], for the building up of the body of Christ, until all come to the unity of the faith and of the knowledge of the Son of God, to maturity, to the measure of the full stature of Christ" (Eph 4:12-13).

The early church presents a truly collaborative vision for ministry: (1) a unity of many ministries tied to one mission; (2) ministries that match gifts of the Spirit in response to the changing needs of God's people; and (3) ministers who collaborate as coworkers in carrying out the mission of God in the world. "Throughout the ages the Holy Spirit makes the entire Church 'one in communion and in ministry and provides her with different hierarchical and charismatic gifts,' . . . inspiring in the hearts of the faithful that same spirit of mission which impelled Christ himself" (AG 4).

That vision of ministry is also at work today. Theological discussions of ministry now identify clear points of convergence with these features of ministry in the early church.[9] First, there is a rich diversity in pastoral ministry. In baptism all are drawn into and given a share in the one mission of Christ. They participate in that mission in particular forms of ministry suited to their calling in life and the rich diversity of gifts the Spirit gives them for carrying out the one mission of the Christ.

Second, the variety of ministries reflects today's context and needs, from ordained ministries to lay ecclesial ministers, ministers of hospitality, bereavement ministers, and ministers of various outreach services such as peace and justice. Naming them today does not fit easily into Paul's categories, though we might still use his "forms of leadership" and "forms of assistance" (1 Cor 12:28) as overarching labels. An ordering of the various ministries begun in the early church continued to be adapted in the past, as it is also doing now.[10]

9. These paragraphs draw on Susan K. Wood's summary of the 2001 Collegeville Ministry Seminar, "Conclusion: Convergence Points toward a Theology of Ordered Ministries," in *Ordering the Baptismal Priesthood: Theologies of Lay and Ordained Ministry*, ed. Susan K. Wood (Collegeville, MN: Liturgical Press, 2003), 256–67.

10. Richard R. Gaillardetz, "The Ecclesial Foundations of Ministry within an Ordered Communion," in Wood, *Ordering the Baptismal Priesthood*, 26–51, recommends thinking of ministry as "ecclesial re-positioning," highlighting an underlying linking of all ministry, and he proposes a

Third, because all ministries are ordered toward achieving the common purpose of the *missio Dei* entrusted first to Christ and then by him to the church, collaboration in the work of guiding his disciples is needed. Kathleen Cahalan notes: "Each minister strives to embody all aspects of ministry in their work because they meet the disciple as disciple"; ministries also require specialization "well suited for the ministers' charisms and the community's good. But that specialized role is never separate from the minister's responsibility to participate in a community in which all aspects of ministry are present. Likewise, in areas where an individual minister is not as well equipped or capable, they work in tandem with others to insure that disciples are well served."[11] They are coworkers in the vineyard.

Ministries, then, are particular ways of carrying out God's mission. They are the ministerial service of "missionary disciples." Some of those ministries bear the official responsibility of providing servant leadership of the community. The focus in this book has been on ministries that involve some degree of leadership of the community as a whole, forming others for their ministerial role in carrying out God's mission. What is important for our purposes is captured in definitions by Cahalan: "Stated simply . . . *ministry is the vocation of leading disciples in the life of discipleship for the sake of God's mission in the world.*"[12] Their role of leadership does not negate their own discipleship: "Ministers are disciples and remain disciples even as ministers. Broadly defined, ministers are disciples who become leaders in the

---

threefold arrangement of that ordering: ordained ministry, installed ministries, and commissioned ministries.

11. Kathleen A. Cahalan, "Toward a Fundamental Theology of Ministry," *Worship* 80, no. 2 (March 2006): 119, 120.

12. Kathleen A. Cahalan, *Introducing the Practice of Ministry* (Collegeville, MN: Liturgical Press, 2010), 50, emphasis original.

community."[13] Their position of leadership is to remain a ministry of service to the others (Matt 23:8-11).[14]

How are mission and ministry related? The initial quotation says it well: "in the church there is diversity of ministry but oneness of mission" (AA 2).

13. Cahalan, "Toward a Fundamental Theology," 116.

14. Alternate language of Vatican II and subsequent documents states very clearly that ministerial priesthood is in service of common priesthood, that ministerial priesthood is based on this common priesthood and ordered to its service (LG 10; CCC 1120, 1547, 1591; John Paul II, Postsynodal Apostolic Exhortation *Pastores Dabo Vobis* [1992], 16, http://www.vatican .va/content/john-paul-ii/en/apost_exhortations/documents/hf_jp-ii _exh_25031992_pastores-dabo-vobis.html.

4 A Reweaving Workshop

The design that follows is based on a workshop I conducted for a large urban parish in which there were well over fifty ministry groups (called "commissions") of various kinds. These commissions served both the internal life of the parish as well as outreach in response to many different needs and issues. Earlier that year, the commissions had each engaged in a process of reflecting on their experience and ways to develop their ministries further. These commissions came together for this day-long workshop to reflect on ways to coordinate their work.

The morning was devoted to reflecting on the Emmaus story in a modified form of *lectio divina*. The goal was to provide an overarching biblical paradigm for coordinating the ministries. Participants were first given a copy of the text with wide margins for them to highlight or annotate the words and phrases that spoke to them about the experience of the two disciples on the way. All were then asked to share aloud the words and phrases they had chosen. Frequent repetitions of the same words and phrases by the participants became a shared chorus highlighting how common aspects of the story had spoken to them.

An extended time of guided reflections on the setting of the story followed.[1] The five major moments/stages in the experience of the two disciples were identified, along with the five ways in which the stranger ministered to them as he companioned them on the way. These moments/stages

---

1. Reflections much like those in chapter 7 or spread throughout the previous chapters.

were named in contemporary language for an integrated
weaving together of pastoral ministries. How these ministries unfolded, each building on the previous one, was
drawn out. Participants were thus enabled to see two important things about their ministries. First, these ministries
are markers along the continuing integral faith journey of
disciples. The priority is ministering as coworkers to that
unfolding journey at particular moments. Second, in the
Emmaus account these ministries are all exercised by the
stranger. Those ministries are now exercised by many who
are acting only in his name. He is the one who baptizes and
teaches when we baptize and teach.[2] Speaking about ministry, Paul says, "we have this treasure in clay jars, so that
it may be made clear that this extraordinary power belongs
to God and does not come from us" (2 Cor 4:7).

The afternoon session consisted of two phases. First, the
commissions each met by themselves to ask the following
questions in light of the Emmaus model of the integrated
unity of the faith journey and ministry to it.

Where does our ministry fit into the Emmaus story?

*How does the Emmaus story confirm and/or challenge our
approach to ministry?*

*How might we want to nuance or expand the Emmaus ap-
proach for our context?*

*How can we coordinate what we do with the other pastoral
ministries?*

Second, all the commissions then returned and gathered
in mixed inter-commission groups. They were tasked to:

---

2. We noted earlier that the *Catechism of the Catholic Church* says the
same thing about catechesis (427).

- identify particular areas in which they and other ministries not represented in the group could be of mutual help to each other;

- highlight perspectives and concerns about ministering to disciples that they had gained in their areas of pastoral ministry and that are worth sharing more broadly with other ministries;

- propose concrete ongoing ways to coordinate their work with that of other ministries; and

- imagine key elements for a working vision of a common goal for all the ministries and an understanding of how each ministry would fit into it.

The workshop concluded with a call for each commission at its next meeting to prepare a proposal for the parish staff outlining their recommendations about implementing the ideas generated at the workshop.[3]

A final word about the workshop. It was set within a larger process. A time of reflective debriefing on each of the ministries preceded the workshop, and the workshop led to a subsequent time of visioning and strategizing by the parish staff for ways to reweave and integrate the ministries. The workshop was designed to start from the ministerial experience of the commissions and to gather and engage the wisdom they had gained from it to pass on for the follow-up work of the parish staff. The reweaving workshop was meant to facilitate that longer process at a nodal moment of moving from experience of the individual commissions toward a rewoven

3. This was meant to invite the commissions to engage the parish leadership in visioning, coordination, and oversight for implementing a coordinated approach to the pastoral ministries. I designed the workshop in consultation with the parish leadership but had not been engaged to do any follow-up on it.

approach to pastoral ministry in which all ministers can truly be coworkers in the Lord's vineyard.

This workshop design is offered here in the modest hope that others may find it helpful in thinking about reweaving the ministries. Such a reweaving will be cause for those who are coworkers in ministry to rejoice together in the harvest gathered for eternal life, for they all share in the sowing and reaping (John 4:36-37; also 1 Cor 3:5-9). How much more will it be cause for the unending rejoicing of the people of God themselves, gathered in for the "wedding feast of the Lamb" (Rev 19:9).